BETRAYAL

BETRAYAL

James Mobley

Heliograph Publishing

Clovis, California

BETRAYAL: NEVER WASTE A SOLDIER. Copyright © 2015 James Mobley

Production Assistance Provided by Heliograph Publishing
An Imprint of HBE Publishing

Layout and cover design by Joshua Muster, Heliograph Publishing

All rights reserved. No part of this book may be used or reproduced in any manner whatsoever without written permission from the publisher, except in the case of brief quotations embodied in critical articles or reviews.

All inquiries should be addressed to:
James Mobley
jamesmobley@comcast.net

Library of Congress Control Number: 2015955405

ISBN 978-1-943050-15-4 Hardcover
ISBN 978-1-943050-14-7 Paperback
ISBN 978-1-943050-16-1 Ebook

Printed in the United States of America
November 2015

This book is dedicated to the persons I love most dearly. My wife of 42 years, Laurel Mobley, my sons Christopher and Daniel Mobley, and my grandchildren Evelyn and Sebastian Mobley.

TABLE OF CONTENTS

FORWARD	1
TOMAHAWK	3
FIRE SUPPORT	7
SAPPER	9
PRELUDE TO ATTACK	11
CONTACT	15
SECURITY TAP	23
CAPTURE	25
CLEANUP	29
COBRAS IN THE ELEPHANT VALLEY	31
THE A SHAU	31
COMBAT ASSAULT	37
GUN RUN	43
EXTRACTION	47
R.E.M.F.	51
CAMP EAGLE	55
THE LAP OF LUXURY	57
GOD AND THE ODD ROCKET	63
BANK SHOT	67
THE LIBRARY	69
ASTRONOMY ON THE PERIMTER	71
UNFRIENDLY FIRE	75
THE BROKEN PEACE SIGN	79
SCHOOL LEARNIN'	81
RESISTANCE	85
A CALL FROM MARS	89
FUCK IT	93

FIELD TRIP	97
FOOT IN MOUTH DISEASE	97
TOM	99
SKY PILOT	101
CAMPING OUT	105
COKE KIDS	113
FRAG FISHING	115
OPERATIONS	117
HOW DO YOU SAY HELLO?	121
ALPHA IS FOR AMBUSH	123
SPARKY	127
QUICK KILL	131
LIGHTNING FLASH	133
DAISY CHAIN	137
OH MY GOD	141
GATHERING VEGTABLES	143
DINNER WITH THE FAMILY	147
NOBODY SEEMS TO KNOW	151
FISHING WITH KIT CARSON	155
BLOWING UP THE TRAIN	159
GARBAGE RUN	165
COMMAND AND CAUTION	173
JOE	175
THE HAI VAN PASS	183
I GOTTA GET OUT OF THIS PLACE	187
OLD MAN	187
THE SACRED WATERING HOLE	189
B-HAM	193
OLD FRIENDS	195
TARGET PRACTICE	197
MEDIVAC	199
EPILOGUE	203

Introduction

I have known Jim Mobley for 50 years. He is like a member of my family, as close as my siblings. We did everything together: Working for my dad in the vineyard, my uncle in the manufacturing plant, my other uncle in the restaurant. We hunted and hiked and laughed and cried together. With our friend, Bryon, we drove to New York and Washington D.C. in the summer of 66. We went to Chicago together for the Democratic Convention. We shared everything.

Except one thing: Vietnam. He went and I didn't.

At Sanger High School in the mid-60s we protested by handing out anti-war leaflets on "Career Day" when military recruiters were on campus. This effort landed us in the principal's office. Later, Jim joined the "Resistance", an organization devoted to the proposition that the draft was immoral and that the way to stop the war was to not just avoid service (by going to college like me, for instance) but by refusing to participate in the system. Jim burned his draft card, refused induction and was indicted by a federal grand jury. Then, I and several other friends of Jim urged him not to wreck his life by going to jail. I don't know why he changed his mind. That is his story to tell.

I wish I still had Jim's letters from Vietnam. They could make up a book by themselves. He didn't have to risk his life in combat.

He had a cushy job as a clerk, out of danger. I remember reading between the lines in those letters. Slowly, inexorably, some force within him led him to the front. Again, that is his story to tell.

The vignettes contained here tell us as much about Jim as about the war: Watching the Cong blow up another train as routinely as you would hear the telephone ring; seeing a woman get her legs blown off while gathering vegetables for her family; befriending a Chu Hoi and learning the ultimate truth of the war by watching him fish; the pleasure he gets from the simple act of saying "Hello" to a family in their own language; and most poignant of all "Dinner with the Family". Jim's act of moral heroism in an instant is no surprise to those of us who know him and in my view justifies his entire experience. Maybe it's what he was sent there to do.

RICK LEHMAN

North Fork California
June, 2011

FORWARD

I am a "grunt" - an infantryman - and a combat veteran. Once you are a grunt, you stay a grunt forever. It's like another skin and you can't take it off. My war was Vietnam. My outfit was 1st Platoon, Alpha Company, 2nd Battalion, 327th Infantry Regiment, 101st Airborne Division: the "Screaming Eagles."

The legend of the 101st goes back to D-Day, June 6th, 1944, when the division jumped, behind enemy lines, into the predawn darkness of Normandy. It continues through the Battle of the Bulge - the largest battle in American military history - where the 101st held off a key element of the final German offensive.  My regiment earned the nickname "The Bastogne Bulldogs" at a critical cross-roads in the Arden forest where they held the line though vastly outnumbered. A generation later they would fight and die to take a 937 meter hill called *Dong Ap Bia* by the Vietnamese. Americans call it "Hamburger Hill."

The 101st fought along with the Marines to defeat the NVA at the Battle of Hue during the TET of 1968. They fought the last major battle of the Vietnam War at a firebase named Ripcord. The Screaming Eagles suffered more casualties in Vietnam than any other infantry division. There is no way to describe to someone who has not served in uniform how proud I am to have been a member of the 101st Airborne Division. There is no need to describe it to my brothers-in-arms.

This is my Vietnam War memoir. The story is 45 years late and I have struggled with the decision to tell it. The War in Vietnam ended for the United States on January 27th, 1973, with the signing of the Paris Peace Accords. It ended for the Vietnamese on April 30th, 1975, when Saigon fell. It ended for me on March 13th, 1971, when I left Vietnam, but no day has passed in the last 45 years when it does not haunt me.

I'm writing this because I have to. Vietnam will not let me rest. Like Ahab's whale, it "tasks me." I may well be as crazy as Melville's character. I am consumed with an unquenchable rage as Ahab was. It is my hope that dumping all this on paper may ease that a little.

The first requirement of this book is that it be true to me. The second requirement of this book is that it be true to my brothers-in-arms. The third requirement of this book is that it be true to my country. I am a veteran of combat on behalf of the United States of America and I need apologize to no-one for what I will say here. This is my Vietnam story.

TOMAHAWK

I woke up in mid-air - in the middle - of an unwinnable war. That I woke up in mid-air is a fact. That the war could not be won is my opinion. That we did not win it is history.

The blast that blew me out of my bunk was from an RPG - a rocket propelled grenade - one of the cheapest and nastiest weapons ever conceived. It was fired at my bunker by a man who had walked all the way from his home in North Vietnam, through the meanest jungle on God's earth, just to attack Fire Support Base Tomahawk. It wasn't personal, of course. He wasn't after me in particular, and it wasn't personal when I killed him. The North Vietnamese Army (NVA) [i] sapper company that attacked Tomahawk was made of tough, determined men who knew that a lot of them would not live. Most of them didn't.

* * *

Tomahawk was on top of a hill rising just west of the village of Phu Loc. It was located right beside the one and only highway running through this part of Vietnam called QL1 or Highway-1. It had a great view of the Gulf of Tonkin to the north, part of the South

China Sea. We could see the fishing boats in the little bay between the mainland and Vin Loc Island, the highway running east to west at the foot of the hill, and the railroad track that tunneled

beneath it. The road with its civilian and military traffic ran beside rice paddies that were next to the villages and hamlets. We had a bird's-eye view of the land and life of the Vietnamese people.

It had another view to the south, but only of jungle. The Bach Ma Mountains, of which Tomahawk was part, rose from the narrow coastal plain. The flat cropland area between the sea and the jungle was so narrow in this part of Vietnam that in places it was only a few hundred yards wide and never more than a few thousand. Where the mountains rose from the lowlands the jungle began. From there, the mountains and jungle extended back, and then further back, forever I think. I called it "the Edge." It was the edge of the jungle. It was the edge of our vision. It was the edge of their domain.

It was covered with double and triple-canopy vegetation where we could see only a few yards or feet into it, and it continued al-

most unbroken until you reached Thailand. It was like a green ocean. The Edge was its shoreline. From the Edge they appeared - to the Edge they disappeared. We never knew when they were coming. They almost always knew when we were coming. I spent many months in that bush and it is one of the reasons I know we could never have won that war. Our enemy was tough but they could not have beaten us without that jungle.

FIRE SUPPORT

Fire Support Bases were established all over our Area of Operations (AO). They were exactly what the name implied. Almost always on a hilltop, denuded down to the dirt, these bases were homes to artillery batteries - the howitzers, mortars and gun crews whose job it was to provide fire support to the infantry.

These bases, together with American airpower, were central to our strategy of attrition through the use of massive fire power. That was the plan the military leadership had for winning the war in Vietnam: kill the enemy until he gave up.

Artillery firebases such as Tomahawk were heavily fortified. They had bunkers and fighting trenches lined with sandbags. There was concertina wire and tangle-foot wire around the perimeter to impede the enemy. There were trip flares, claymore mines and 55 gallon drums of Napalm. The upper part of the hill was cleared of anything that might provide cover for the enemy. And then they had us (the infantry) defending the perimeter. As grunts, we had our M-16s,

TOMAHAWK PERIMITER

M-60 machine guns, grenade launchers and hand grenades, and, we held the high ground. It wasn't the sort of place you would ordinarily want to attack. When they did, it was for a very specific reason. They planned well but knew they would suffer heavy casualties. They judged the goals to be worth the price and they paid it.

SAPPER

The early hours of June 10th, 1970, the day before my 22nd birthday, were pitch black. The moon had set by 22:00 the previous night. There was only starlight.

We were uphill, fortified, and loaded for a siege. The NVA were below us, crawling towards our position, slipping through rows of wire, almost naked, carrying only a bag of TNT satchel charge explosives and an AK47 assault rifle or an RPG.

These were "Sappers" (commandos) and they could only overcome such defenses as ours through stealth and surprise. Dressed only in a loin cloth or a pair of shorts, bodies blackened, a sapper's method was to crawl on his belly, penetrate our perimeter undetected, and then quickly run from bunker to bunker tossing in his satchel charges before the defenders could react. It was a very dangerous tactic. Done correctly - and with luck - it is a devastating attack.

Almost exactly a year earlier, on June 19th 1969, NVA sappers had successfully overrun this same firebase. The artillerymen - C Battery, 1/138th Field Artillery [ii] - and the 101st grunts defending the perimeter - 3rd platoon of Delta Company, 501st Infantry [iii] - were decimated. Of the fifty-four troops on the hill, only one escaped without injury and thirteen were killed-in action (KIA).

On this night a year later, on what was now my god-damned hill, the lead sappers were already through the wire. They were seconds away from success. But, there were two major differences from the attack of 1969. This time, the weather was perfectly clear and, most critically, we held the high ground.

PRELUDE TO ATTACK

Captain Bob Cox had been troubled the night before. He was commanding Delta Company, 2/327th Infantry, and was "King of the Hill", as the infantry commander on a firebase was called, responsible for the defense of the hill. His Command Post (CP) was temporarily on Tomahawk and his 3rd Platoon was securing the perimeter. Delta's 2nd Platoon was in the bush a half kilometer to the south-west, and 1st Platoon was ambushing along the railroad track to the north-east. He had not been briefed about the devastating attack on Tomahawk one year earlier. There was no intelligence that an attack was imminent. Captain Cox was about two weeks short of going home.

Captain Cox was uneasy. Delta Company had a mixture of guys in all different phases of their tours like all the units in Vietnam. Some had been there almost a year and had their shit together. Others were pure cherry and had not seen any actual combat yet and the rest were somewhere in the middle.

CAPTAIN COX & 1ST SGT. DEARMAN

He was especially concerned about the second group because of how long things had been quiet. The new guys frankly didn't know - yet - how dangerous a place this was. Everyone was on his own 12 month countdown. It was an insane policy in an insane war. Experience and unit cohesion were destroyed in an effort by the government to minimize the war to the American public. After all, it was only one year we had to make it through, and then we could return to our normal lives. Right?

Call it instinct or blind luck, but on the night of June 8th, Capt. Cox couldn't sleep. He got out of his bunk and decided to take a walk to check the perimeter. What he found pissed him off so badly that he ended up slamming his helmet to the ground and cursing a blue streak at the unfortunate troopers he caught showing slack in "No Slack." Some had not yet connected the hand detonators to the wires that led to the claymore mines. These were the first things you would fire in the event of an attack.

One soldier was sitting on top of his bunker. When Capt. Cox asked him where his weapon was, he pointed to the M-16 that was a dozen feet away from him down in the fighting trench. Another was sleeping in front of his bunker - not on the safe side behind the sandbags but between the front of the position and the wire where he was completely exposed. Needless to say, the perimeter was considerably sharpened up after his midnight tour. Capt. Cox called a meeting of his sergeants and squad leaders the next morning and chewed out their collective asses. The perimeter was extra alert the following night - the night of the attack.

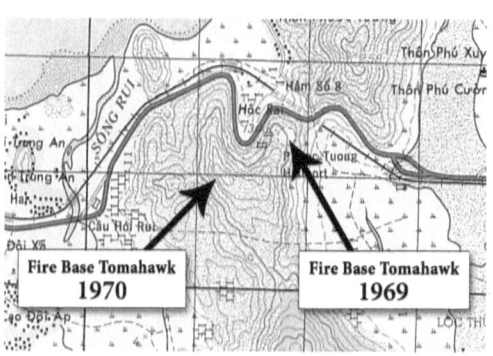

Viewed from above, T-Hawk was shaped a bit like a crab's claw. Two spurs of the hill ran to the north towards the highway and these "claws" seemed to pinch the road into a "V" shape. The eastern of these claws was where the road up to the hill was located. The western claw was bare and cleared of vegetation for about 100 yards in front of the wire. This was where they chose to attack us.

It was one of the same approaches they used the year before. However, in 1969 the firebase was 80 meters lower and 500 meters to the north-east of our current position, right next to Highway 1. The guys from C Battery knew they were in a bad location.^{iv} There was high ground on two sides of the gun positions; one across the road and the other rising to their south-west which allowed the sappers to approach them from above and unseen.

I can't imagine a sane explanation for ignoring centuries of military knowledge and placing the Infantry and Artillery on the old Tomahawk in such clear danger. However the blunder occurred, after the disastrous attack in 1969, the 101st immediately moved the firebase to the top of the hill where it belonged in the first place and where I found myself this night a year later.

The sappers' approach was aimed straight at bunker 7. Bunker 7 was centered on the spur just below the top of the hill, about 10 yards behind the edge of the wire. For me, it was "lucky bunker 7." Walter Washington, Ron Huffines and Bobby Flannery were manning bunker 7 and they were not cherries. They had all been in combat together and knew about staying alert.

I don't believe in fate or divine intervention, but I am certain of the law of unintended consequences. Several months before, these same three squad members had been ambushing at night in the lowlands. Huffines had been pissed off at Washington because he laid back down after Ron passed the watch to him. Before Ron could crawl over to him to give him some shit, four VC walked right into their position. Huffines killed the first VC at a range of a few feet with a reflexive burst. Bobby Flannery, who was face to face with the second, butt-stroked him and knocked him out cold. The last two were fired up by other guys in the platoon and killed. This was great. They had a body count and a prisoner. Capt. Cox was pleased and Sgt. Washington would never lie back down on guard again. As it turned out, Walter Washington was the alert soldier on T-Hawk who first spotted the enemy by that starlight.

The next morning, Cox called for a helicopter to take his POW prize to the rear. The slick arrived and (the story blurs a little here) something happened. As they were about to load the prisoner into the chopper, Bobby Flannery shot and killed the VC. The official story is that Flannery thought the VC was trying to escape and bumped into him. He swears he did not know that the prisoner's hands and feet were bound. His commander had the authority to do a lot of different things including sanctions that would have removed him from the field and, if he was a real ass-hole, even charges. If he had, Flannery wouldn't have been on T-Hawk to fire a critical recoilless rifle round and throw hand grenades at the Sappers just as they were breaching the wire.

CONTACT

After midnight, Sgt. Washington was scanning the ridge to his front using a large, tripod mounted starlight scope called a "night observation device" (NOD). Using only the available starlight, the device allowed you to see at night in a kind of grizzly green light.

A little after 1:30 am, he saw movement - lots of movement - in the wire. 70 NVA commandos were poised to begin their final rush against the 22 guys of 3rd platoon. The wire had been cut, much of the defensive ordinance had been disabled, and my life expectancy was down to a couple of minutes.

Sgt. Washington called the command post on the land line to alert Capt. Cox. A star cluster flare was launched to briefly illuminate the wire and confirm Walter's report. The sappers all went flat - not being sure that the flare was for them or something else. Then a second flare was fired and there was no longer any doubt. They had been found out. They had no choice. They opened fire with everything they had. It was 0140.

Their first RPG barrage was against bunker 7 and the ammo dump about 50 yards further around the hill. The guys on bunker 7 were shaken and the chain link fence in front of them - designed to explode an RPG early - had a big hole in it.. The ammo dump was obliterated. There was simply nothing there anymore but blackened ground.

Ron Huffines opened fire with his M-16 and, part way through his first magazine, his rifle jammed. He calls it his "miracle jam." He crouched down in the fighting position to clear the weapon when he realized there was a whole case of hand grenades at his feet. He put down the M16 and began his own artillery barrage as fast as he could pull the pins on the frags and toss them at the enemy.

At the same time, Bob Flannery detonated the claymore mines in front of his position and joined in with his own hand grenade barrage from his fighting position to the right of Huffines. He saw an RPG team inside the perimeter right in front of him. They were reloading the RPG to fire on his position when he killed them both. He says they got within 10 feet. He also fired the 90mm recoilless rifle lying beside his fighting position. It was the modern bazooka and it was loaded with an anti-personnel rocket called a flachette round.

REMAINS OF AMMO DUMP

This ammunition consisted of a canister loaded with several

thousand little steel darts - sort of a mega-shotgun. [v] Bunker 7 was the gateway to the rest of the hill and the NVA had to take it out first. The three guys manning it pretty much saved all of our lives by detecting and then repelling the initial attack.

After the initial contact, the whole hill came alive. The bunkers to the left and right of bunker 7 joined the firefight as the NVA who were exposed at the edge of the wire assaulted the hill with grim desperation. If they could get inside, they still might fulfill their mission. Otherwise, they knew they were all dead.

It was on their second volley that my bunker was hit. I was asleep when the rocket slammed into it. The RPG is an inexpensive way to turn anyone over the age of 8 into a tank killer. Or a bunker-buster.

The rocket hit the side of my bunker on the opposite side of the three sandbag wall I was lying next to. It only went through two and a half sandbags. I was asleep on the top of a wooden bunk bed. The concussion jarred the bunk so hard that it threw me straight sideways several feet, still prone, face down. I woke up staring down at the floor.

I recall the impression of being suspended in the air for a long moment. Then, the floor seemed to rise up to me in slow motion and hit me in the chest. I didn't feel a thing. It was one of those moments that you experience in a near miss car accident - or any sudden, violent danger, when the human brain shifts into a higher speed. Before this, I did not know a human being could wake up that quickly. In the time - in between the time - you drop a ball and it begins to fall.

I jumped up, grabbed my weapon, steel pot and ammo, and crawled outside to the fighting trench. A staff sergeant was right on my heels. Gunfire and concussions seemed to be everywhere. The mortars were beginning to put up illumination rounds with that eerie yellow light that comes from parachute flares. The hill was on fire and the whole world was exploding. I deduced we were under attack.

This is the same moment we lost Birch Udell Stemmons. Attached to the 101st artillery unit on T-hawk as a ground surveillance radar crewman, he was from Columbia, Missouri and was 5 months younger than me. He was killed when the tail fin of one of our parachute flares embedded itself in his skull. Death was instantaneous. In the chaos and confusion of the first moments of the attack, the mortar crew had fired in haste at a bad angle. Birch was at his post - doing his duty - when he gave his life for his country. He was one of three casualties on the American side and the only KIA.

The NVA soldier who fired the RPG at me was on the lower knoll to our west that stood between us and Phu Loc. Across the draw between the two hills, he was maybe seventy-five meters away. I think he was supposed to wait until all his men were through the wire and then provide fire support from outside the perimeter. He was forced shoot early because they had been discovered and his comrades were being cut down. The sergeant and I saw the muzzle flash on the hillside opposite our position in the same instant.

"Did you see that?" I asked him as I got off my first shot. "Yeah" he said as he opened fire a half-second later.

We both emptied our magazines at the point of the flash and the position was silenced. The sergeant found the guy during the sweep the next morning with a hole in his forehead. I got the first shot off so the sergeant agreed it was my kill. He had others that day and could afford to be generous.

Two minutes later, we watched another firefight erupt below us in the village of Phu Loc. A different NVA unit was attacking the tactical operations center (TOC) located there. The red tracers were going one way and green tracers were going the other. Rockets and mortars were impacting inside the TOC compound and we knew that this fight was bigger than just our hill. Six minutes after that, they opened up on Firebase Los Banos, eight kilometers to our east. Eight minutes after that, another enemy unit attacked the bridge at Nuoc Ngot, one kilometer to our east. The attack turned out to be a battalion sized NVA operation with coordinated attacks on four 101st installations within the Phu Loc district launched at 0140, 0144, 0150, and 0158. Pretty good coordination using those cheap Chinese watches.

Shortly after the attack began, Lt. Daniel Sherman, who was responsible for our section of the perimeter, came up behind our position crouching low. He was uphill from us and would have presented a silhouette if he stood erect.

"You guys O.K. here?" "Yes sir!" we replied. "Watch for gooks inside the perimeter," he said. Then we started looking behind us as well as to our front.

Sherman was good example of the crazy policies of higher command. A good field commander leading 2nd platoon, he had been reassigned after 6 months to become the battalion S4 (supply officer). He was the reason I was on the hill that day. He needed a mule driver to move supplies around the hill and I volunteered from where I was in the rear when they asked who would like to go to Tomahawk. This 6 month field time limit was applied to all platoon leaders and company commanders to make way for other officers who needed to log their field time. Just as they became really experienced, the field commanders were replaced by cherries. Lessons learned were forgotten and mistakes were repeated because the institutional memory kept turning over. It was military madness.

* * *

The firefight probably only lasted about 15 minutes, but it seemed like it was all night. After the guys on bunker 7 stopped the initial assault - none of the NVA made it beyond their position - artillery support began carpeting the area around the hill with cluster rounds. These were mini-bombs packed inside a 155mm artillery round that burst just before the shell struck the ground and scattered its anti-personnel bomblets.

Captain Cox called in an airstrike and two F4 Phantom jets from a carrier in the gulf passed so low over our heads I think I could have hit one with a rock. Loud doesn't begin to describe the noise. They dropped 4 napalm canisters on the ridge a couple of hundred yards to our south-east which erupted into those incredible bright red spreading blossoms of fire that must have been designed in hell. The ridge was the enemies escape route. I don't know how many were consumed in that conflagration but it had to be a bunch. Often, we never found out such things. Sometimes our patrols would come upon a dead enemy long after they were killed.

Because T-Hawk was high on a hill, our battle could be seen all over the Phu Loc AO. By all accounts it was quite a lightshow from a distance. Platoons from Alpha, Delta, Bravo and others in sight of T-Hawk - some as close as half a klic (kilometer) away - could only watch the spectacle as it unfolded. The explosion of the ammo dump, the RPG impacts, the lights from the flares, the small arms tracers from rifles and machine guns (red for us, green for them), the napalm attack by the F-4 Phantom jets, the artillery cluster rounds exploding around the perimeter.

It all played out before them like a surreal movie - terrible and beautiful. In the morning after the attack, converging on the vicinity of the battle, several units encountered some of the leftovers from the enemy who made it away from the hill. Some of these were killed and some were captured. Altogether, it's fair to say the attacking force was effectively wiped out.

SECURITY TAP

When the sun came up, we went outside the wire to sweep for survivors. I fell in behind 1st Sgt. Dearman. It just seemed like the thing to do at the time. Within a few paces, we came upon the first of the not quite yet dead. A South Vietnamese (ARVN) soldier standing next to the Sergeant was just a couple of meters ahead of me. He leaned over the wounded man and was screaming in his face. I had no idea what he was saying but it had the tone of curses. Maybe the NVA killed his best friend or something. The sapper's mouth moved in response but I couldn't hear him. Then, the Kit Carson stood up straight, pointed his M-16 at the sappers face, and pulled the trigger. At 700 rounds-a-minutes, it takes a little under 3 seconds to empty a 30 round magazine. He didn't stop until it was empty. Once again, that damned slowing of time made it seem like about 3 minutes watching the sapper's head dissolve - bone chips and brains in a Cuisinart. When the magazine was empty, all that really remained was the lower jaw and a pile of pink goo with what looked like egg shells mixed in.

Two more steps and the staff sergeant to my 10 o'clock and about 5 meters away - the same Sgt. who was with me in the trench during the firefight - yelled back to the master sergeant, "Sarge! There's a gook! What do I do?" The top sergeant snapped back instantly, "kill him." I looked where he was pointing his rifle and there sat an older sapper - probably an officer. I could not see if he had anything in his lap because he had his back to us - facing towards the South China Sea. He was rocking back and forth, and it seemed to me that he was praying in the custom of the Buddhists. Two seconds later the staff sergeant snapped three quick rounds through his back - good shots, center mass, tight group - and the sapper fell slowly and gently to his left and died.

CAPTURE

At this point, I turned right when the squad turned left. I started my own sweep in the opposite direction. I had to do my duty and clear the hill but I didn't have to follow that meat grinder. There was an un-cleared area just to the right (east) of the attack ridge. It was on a shelf that was tucked under a nearly vertical drop-off below the bunker line above. This made it out-of-sight to the men above unless they leaned over the sandbags and looked straight down.

Descending down the sloop into this area, I moved cautiously in spite of the fact that I was stupid and alone. I was doing what is called "recon by fire." If there was even the tiniest bush that could conceal a sapper, I fired a burst into it before looking behind it.

At first, I didn't see the sapper directly in front of me. He was hunkered in a fetal position, head down, in a little crater hole with only his back showing. His skin was the color of the ground. If I had taken two or three more steps, I would have walked onto his back.

When I did spot him, I took two quick steps back. I was ready to kill him but he wasn't moving or doing anything except keeping real still, probably hoping he hadn't been seen. So, I shouted, "dừng lại." It was one of maybe a dozen phrases I had learned during the orientation you go through when you first arrive in country. It means "halt" in Vietnamese. It was not a good choice of words, since he was quite motionless, but it was a close as I could get to "don't move."

I guess because I used words instead of just firing him up, he very slowly raised his head and looked me in the eyes. I motioned for him to stand up. He was stark naked. My 16 was on full rock-and-roll, leveled at the center of his chest, but, unless he had a frag stuffed up his ass cheeks, I concluded he was unarmed. I shouted over my shoulder to the bunker above, "Hey! I've got a prisoner! Send me an interpreter." In just a few seconds, another ARVN came scurrying down the hill. Apparently he either didn't have the same personal grudge against the NVA that his partner did, or else he recognized the value of intelligence gathered from POWs. Even before he reached us, he was talking in soft, reassuring tones and he kept it up as he hurried up to us. Then, he literally took the sapper by the hand and led him slowly to the top of the hill. I followed close behind in case the sapper decided to stop giving up.

When we got to the CP, I turned him over to the Delta guys outside who were already guarding two other prisoners. One of the POWs looked angry and defiant, one looked like he was in shock, and the one I captured never changed the flat expression on his face. The five or six grunts from Delta Co. who were guarding the prisoners looked like they wanted them to move.

The POW's were stunned, forlorn and pissed off, but they were alive and a source of useful intelligence. I hope my POW went on to have grandchildren.

Opposite is a picture of my prisoner with Captain Cox (facing the POW) along with Delta Dog (at the prisoner's feet) and some brass who had come to the hill to take credit. Delta Dog was the hill mutt who was named thus because Delta Co. was currently on the hill. Captain Cox told me he saw Delta Dog trotting around proudly after the battle with the dismembered hand of a sapper in his mouth.

After turning over the POW, I just roamed around the hill for a while in a strange out-of-body state of mind. I saw another sapper who was wrapped up in the concertina wire on the south side of the hill. I don't know if he was alive. The wire had been blown into a tangled pile and the sapper was actually suspended off the ground several feet. He was so wrapped up in the razor wire that it was hard to tell where the wire ended and he began. An officer put a round through his head with his 45 side arm - just in case. That was the third "security tap" I saw that day. I won't judge the decisions made by those soldiers in the heat of the moment but I know we could have captured more than we did.

CLEANUP

The cleanup didn't take very long. Most of the NVA bodies were clustered in front of bunker 7 and the grunts had collected them on the upper chopper pad. I drove the mule back and forth between the upper pad and the lower, main chopper pad where the bodies were being thrown into a pile until all twenty-eight sappers were stacked willy-nilly. In my mind, the pile looked like it was as high as I was tall. I saw one trooper climb on top of the pile so he could have his picture taken with his rifle raised over his head in triumph. I thought it was in poor taste at the time but I wish I had a copy today.

A short time later, a truck arrived and the bodies were taken down to the highway where they were tossed onto the side of the road for the locals to deal with. Captain Cox told me many years later that he regretted the manner in which the Americans handled the enemy dead.

I found out only recently that the NVA were buried by the local residents in a cemetery created at the foot of Tomahawk. Their remains were treated with dignity in the end. We lost one guy. They lost most of a company though some surely escaped to fight another day. Most of us went home after a year. They stayed and fought until they died. Or won.

COBRAS IN THE ELEPHANT VALLEY

THE A SHAU

The door-gunner leaned toward me and shouted over the noise of the chopper. "It's hot!" He was wearing one of those really cool door-gunner helmets with the completely black face shield that made him look like a spaceman. With the word "hot," I turned to look at him. I couldn't see the expression on his face through the face shield but I knew he wasn't referring to the weather. He had just heard over his headset that there was enemy contact at our landing zone (LZ). An airmobile combat assault (CA) into a "hot" LZ (enemy fire in progress) is pretty much every grunt's nightmare. I passed the word to the next man who passed it to the next. All of

DEC 25, 1970

us took our muzzle covers off and readied ourselves.

We were on a CA (again) riding in a UH-1 ("Huey") helicopter that we called a "slick." All rucked-up with our full battle gear, our legs dangled over the jungle as we flew a thousand feet over the waves of the green ocean - that damned green ocean that went on from horizon to horizon.

No matter where you looked, it was mountainous jungle and you couldn't see shit on the ground. Sitting on the edge of the slick and looking all around from my lofty viewpoint, I really wondered in that moment how they picked the places they sent us. Was some Coronel scouting high up in his Charlie-Charlie bird (command and coordination helicopter) and sticking pins in a map on a hunch? The regular riflemen - PFCs and Spec4s like me - almost never knew where we were going or what awaited us.

We did this all the time. On an hour's notice, command would send a flight of slicks to carry our platoon on a CA. This means picking you up somewhere where you are safe for the moment and transporting your platoon somewhere that wasn't. Since our platoon was never at full strength, we usually needed only three birds that could carry up to eight men each (plus the aircrew).

On this CA, we were headed to the Elephant Valley, the northern-most finger of the A Shau Valley. The A Shau was a place of dread for any grunt who had been there or who knew anyone that had. It was the major waypoint for the NVA in our area of operations. They accessed it via a major off-ramp of the Ho Chi Minh trail and used it to stockpile men, weapons and supplies. There were warehouses, troop barracks, field hospitals, communication lines, even R&R centers, scattered throughout the A Shau. They were dug underground or into hillsides and so well camouflaged you couldn't see any of it unless you fell in. It was the main infiltration route for the NVA and VC attack on the ancient imperial capital of Hue that was launched in the Tet of '68.

The Ho Chi Minh trail and the A Shau Valley warehouses they fed had to be destroyed for the United States to win the Vietnam War. From the late 1950s through the middle of 1970, Americans did everything they could do to deny the enemy this strategic supply center and staging area.

At our peak effort, Air Force and Navy aircraft conducted as many as a hundred sorties per day against the Ho Chi Minh trail [vi] killing untold thousands of North Vietnamese who were carrying supplies from Russia and China to the South. These individual Vietnamese porters numbered in the hundreds of thousands. They used trucks, elephants, bicycles, and their backs. They were North Vietnam's second army, and nothing we did could permanently stop them. In the end, the best we could do was slow them down or make them pause briefly while they created new trails to the valley. Then, the supply train resumed.

Early on, there were efforts by the CIA working with indigenous Montangnards [vii] to fight the NVA for control of the valley. The Montangnards were driven out but the NVA remained. In the early '60s, US Military "advisors" leading South Vietnamese troops tried to clear the Valley with no better success.

After that, frontline American combat divisions took over the mission. The 1st Marine Division, the 1st Cavalry Division, and, finally, the 101st Airborne Division tried to force the enemy out of the A Shau. The NVA's strategy hinged on the fiercest possible defense of this supply cache. Although we killed many thousands of the enemy soldiers and captured or destroyed thousands of tons of supplies, we couldn't find all of their stuff or kill all of their soldiers. The A Shau remained full of material in spite of the best efforts of the combined allied forces.

The Elephant Valley was a narrow gash at the north end of the A Shau. At its widest it was less than a kilometer across and it was surrounded on all sides by steep, jungle-covered mountains.

A year before, 6 kilometers to the southwest of our current destination, a battle was fought for a mountain named Dong Ap Bia. On the map, it was designated Hill 937 (it's height in meters), but, as I said before, Americans know it as "Hamburger Hill." The enemy occupied the hill and the US high command made the decision to prove a point. They ordered a frontal infantry assault against an enemy dug in hard on the high ground. After seven attempts over ten days, the Screaming Eagles finally took the hill. The 101st suffered 456 casualties, including 56 dead. The NVA suffered 630 dead. At the time, we never knew the number of their wounded in this or any other battle. This was a kill ratio of ten to one. Command called it victory and gave the hill back to the NVA. Their only measure of success was the enemy body count. They just knew that Hanoi would get discouraged, or eventually run out of men and give up. They say insanity is repeating the same actions over and over and expecting different results.

Two months before our combat assault this day, the last major battle of the Vietnam War was fought at a firebase named Ripcord [viii] 12 kilometers to the northeast of our target LZ. The 101st constructed Ripcord as part of Operation Texas Star which was officially an attempt to:

"provide territorial security for the accomplishment of pacification and development in the populated lowlands; deny the

enemy access to the populace and resources in the coastal areas; and to seek out and destroy enemy forces, base areas, and cache sites." [ix]

Fact was, we were trying to buy time for the South Vietnamese to get their act together because we were leaving and our government needed "Vietnamization" [x] to be seen as working.

On Ripcord, we occupied the high ground and some surrounding positions, but, the NVA was not going to give up this ground without an all-out fight. They sent two full divisions (twenty-five thousand men) against the fewer than 700 Americans on and around Ripcord. For three weeks in July of 1970, the defenders of Ripcord suffered a vicious siege. They were hit with constant rocket and mortars attacks, sapper attacks, and even human wave attacks. Ripcord was evacuated on July 23rd and the hill was pounded into a moonscape by B52s. The US forces

lost 247 killed. The NVA lost 2,400. Some argue that this final, large-scale, American battle of the war delayed the ultimate defeat of the South by several months and that's probably true. In the end, the Ho Chi Minh trail stayed in business. The story of Ripcord would be suppressed by the Army for 25 years. They didn't want any more lousy press after Hamburger Hill.

COMBAT ASSAULT

You can hear a helicopter coming from a long way off. This is how we snuck up on the enemy. I'm not saying that we never caught the enemy by surprise, but we sure as hell didn't sneak up on them very often. They're the ones who did most of the sneaking. They snuck up on us when they chose to attack and snuck away so we couldn't kill them. Some think this was cowardly, but they were just playing "rope-a-dope."

The American military command established the strategy of "search and destroy" in 1965, but what they were really counting on was "bait and obliterate." We were the bait. This is what a "Combat Assault" was all about. The idea was to force contact with the enemy and then expend enormous firepower from artillery, jets and helicopter gunships while the infantry tried to keep their heads down.

This was not the fire and maneuver of WWII. The Infantry's traditional tactic is "Find, Fix and Finish." The reality in Vietnam was, more often, to stumble onto or be thrust into a position where contact was initiated, thus "finding" the enemy. Then the platoon leader would radio headquarters and they would spend several million dollars on massive firepower of all sorts. The enemy knew this (of course) and, after a "hit-and-run attack," were usually well away from the targeting. Mostly we just blew up jungle. They just kept bleeding us of resources. The death of a thousand cuts.

* * *

The flight had lasted an unusually long time, headed west toward higher mountains and denser jungle, and we knew we were going deep into Indian country. We were about 3 minutes out when  the door gunner warned us that the Hunter-Killer team ahead of us was in contact with the enemy at our LZ. A Hunter-Killer team - also called a "Pink" team - consisted of a light observation helicopter and a Cobra gunship working as a team to locate and destroy the enemy.

At 2 minutes out we could see the Cobra firing up the tree line with his minigun and rockets. A Cobra gunship is a fearful instrument. They were specificaly designed for Vietnam to replace the slicks that were the original close support gunships. The Hueys were too slow and too big with that big, bulbous "shoot me" nose and windows.

The Cobra was none of that. Only as wide as a man's shoulders,  with the pilot in the backseat and the gunner in the front, they were very fast and made a nose-on attack with a profile that someone described as a leaf coming at you edgewise. They were very hard to hit, and they hit very hard.

The Cobras were armed to the teeth with rockets, a 40mm grenade launcher and, best of all, a minigun that could fire 3,000 rounds a minute. Watching a Cobra workout at night was a sight to behold. It looked like a red snake whipping down from the blackness. The stream of fire lashing the ground looked unbroken, but in truth only every 10th round was a tracer. At 50 rounds a second you couldn't tell.

We could see that red snake now - in the daylight - firing up the south edge of the LZ we were about to land on. Actually, land is not the right word. On a hot LZ, the Huey pilots did not touch down. They came down sharply and hovered 3 or 4 feet above the ground. We had to jump off. It's not a terribly long way, unless you are wearing a hundred pounds of gear. My biggest fear at that moment - being a pretty skinny guy - was that I would break an ankle when I hit the ground and become a casualty. I braced myself and stepped off the skid.

I landed just fine. My ankles must have gotten stronger from humping that ruck. The first thing I did when I hit the ground was look for cover. There wasn't any. This was a large LZ and it looked like it had been used before. There was a little low grass and nothing else close for me to hide behind. I popped the quick release on my ruck, tossed it in front of me, and dove behind it.

100 yards to my front, the Cobra continued to rake the tree line. The "Dinks" (the nicest name we ever called them) were busy melting away in the face of the minigun and rocket fire. They knew the next thing was an artillery barrage and an air strike by carrier-based jets. They also knew America had been withdrawing troops for more than a year. They could wait.

So, here we were in one of the worst places in Vietnam, halfway between Hamburger Hill and Ripcord. There were thousands of

NVA within a few miles of us, and some a good deal closer. Lieutenant Dahlgren moved us to the tree line on the west side of the valley. He sternly reminded us to watch our combat spacing and noise discipline.

The Cobra finally broke off and we headed north up the valley. We had to follow the trail because it was the only way to move, other than down the middle of the open center of the valley (which would be suicide).

You never wanted to follow a trail. We didn't build it and you knew you were being watched. As if to put a loud "fuck you, G.I.s" on it, we came to a slight widening of the trail and the point-man motioned for a sudden stop. There, by the trail side, was a cup of rice. That wasn't the bad part. It was still warm.

The NVA trail watchers were either careless or they wanted to send us a message. "We're watching you. We are very close." Then, it started to rain, and visibility that wasn't good to begin with went totally to hell. I don't think I've ever been more afraid. We were at most 20 guys. They could take us whenever they wanted.

The platoon moved slowly, quietly, cautiously down the trail for a couple of hours as the valley continued to narrow. I remember it now as a long, green tunnel only occasionally breaking above us to reveal the sky or to our right to give us a glimpse of the valley floor. The rain letup a little about the same time we were reaching the end of the valley. The LT decided it was time to setup an NDP (night defensive perimeter).

He chose to climb straight up the side of a very steep and muddy hill. To say that it was a difficult climb doesn't do it justice. Two little steps forward and then you slipped three steps backward. We grabbed whatever vegetation we could to pull ourselves up. I had to use my M-16 as a crutch. We helped one another, pulling or pushing passed the worst of it. After an hour of intense struggle, we finally crested the top of the hill.

It was a bitch of a climb, but the LT chose well. Our small platoon could hold off a large force from our position, dug in on the high ground. I started to feel a bit safer. It would take hundreds of enemy troops to take this hill.

GUN RUN

Our platoon sergeant, Bill Beasley, saw the observation helicopter drop smoke at the base of our hill and immediately knew we were in trouble. I didn't see the smoke but I could see the Cobra. My first thought was, "Oh, good. There's a Cobra nearby. Nobody will fuck with us with him around." Then the gunship made that elegant ballet of a turn and pointed his nose directly at us.

A Cobra setting up for a gun run is a beautiful thing to watch. It's a bit like the dive bombers you see in the WWII documentaries "peeling off" with that graceful wingover maneuver that turns in to an attack dive. A Cobra gunship makes a very similar turn except they first pull-up slightly. This has the effect of slowing down the sound of the rotor blades for a moment. Then the pilot rolls the helicopter until the rotors are almost perpendicular to the ground, turns 90 degrees and points his nose down toward his target at about a 45 degree angle. You hear the sound of the blades get faster and faster. The increasing pitch seems to say "I'm coming for you." Even if you have your eyes closed, you can tell from the sound that a Cobra gunship is turning to attack. Now I was thinking "what in the hell is he doing?"

Then, he opened up with his rockets and I knew exactly what he was doing. He was trying to kill us. The Hunter-Killer team believed they were in a free-fire zone, and that the little ants they saw below - that would be us - were the bad guys.

This was one of those moments in war when you slip into a different thought zone and develop tunnel vision. I can't remember seeing the actions of any other members of my platoon. My attention was riveted on the Cobra. I got behind the biggest tree nearest to me and started digging at the outside my ruck for a signal flare.

The Cobra was being systematic. Starting at the base of the hill where the observation helicopter dropped his smoke marker, each two-rocket volley was higher up the hill than the previous. He was walking the rocket fire up the hill in a methodical sweep which would end at the summit. During the last phase of the attack run, the Cobra gunner opened up with the minigun. When a high velocity round goes by you, you hear a loud crack as the round breaks the sound barrier. Now I heard 50 cracks per second. Imagine you are in China-town in San Francisco during the New Year celebration with a hundred young men lighting strings of firecrackers all at once, but faster.

The gunship pulled up at the end of the gun run and began to circle back for the next attack run. By now, I had grabbed one of my star clusters. Every grunt carried a couple of these pyrotechnic signal flares that burst into a shower of colored sparks at their apex. The eleven inch-long aluminum tubes had a cap with a firing pin inside its base. On the opposite end of the tube was a percussion cap like the ones on the casing of a bullet. You remove the cap, put it on the other end so the firing pin is positioned below the percussion cap, aim the tube skyward, and smack the base on something. A charge about the size of a 12 gauge shotgun blasts the flare into the sky. I slammed in down on my knee hard. It hurt.

As my star cluster shot into to sky, it was quickly followed by two or three more from other guys in the platoon. We were shouting at the Cobra that we were the good guys. The enemy would never mark their position. The gunship was just starting his third run at the summit where we were clustered, when he broke off the attack.

The platoon suffered a few minor wounds from shrapnel and debris but nothing critical. Doc was able to handle it until we got back to base camp. It's a miracle no one was killed. They could have fired directly at the top of the hill on the first pass and wiped out the platoon. There may have been some element of doubt in the Cobra crew's minds.

Memory is different for each man. I remember two-gun runs by the Cobra. Others remember one or three. I am certain about the minigun burst and some others don't remember it at all. We didn't talk about the "friendly fire" incident at the time. In war, grunts don't talk about the last danger or the next. If anything at all was said, it was probably "It don't mean 'nuthin'." This requires an answer-response like in church. The correct response is "It don't mean a god-damned thing." For conversation, you talked about how soon you were going home - not the things that might prevent that.

EXTRACTION

After the Cobra left, the rain returned and made it impossible for helicopters to come and get us. We spent several tense days and nights stuck on that hilltop. The NVA absolutely for certain knew we were there after the Cobra attack. They left us alone. American's had been going home for more than a year and they could be patient.

Getting out of the A Shau was our priority as soon as the rain stopped. We descended the side of the hill until we reached the floor of the valley. At the first, reasonably open, flat spot, the LT set us to clearing a landing zone. The brush and little trees were cleared using our machetes, but some of the trees in this spot were too thick and we were in something of a hurry.

Not all explosions are unwelcome. I sort of had an affinity for explosions anyway. They are always exciting, and, if you are the author of the explosion, it can actually be quite satisfying. If it gets you out of the A Shau Valley, it's downright heart-warming.

Every member of the platoon carried at least two pounds of the powerful explosive C-4. We also carried many feet of detonation cord, a thin, plastic-sheathed explosive rope used to link one explosive charge to another in a series that we called a "daisy chain." Unlike dynamite or even TNT, C-4 has a much faster expansion velocity - thirty-thousand feet per second. That's ten times faster than a fast rifle bullet. It is more of a cutting or shattering charge than a pushing charge like dynamite.

C-4 is so powerful that you can cut down a small tree just by wrapping it with several loops of det-cord alone and setting it off with a blasting cap. For larger trees, you can use part of the 1 pound bricks of the plastic explosive which you can tear apart and mold like a stiff clay.

We placed the C-4 and det-cord at the base of a dozen trees that had to be downed to allow a helicopter to land. We linked them together with det-cord strung from tree to tree, and placed the master blasting cap into the nearest charge. That blasting cap was at the end of an electric cord that looked like it could be attached to your living room lamp. The other end was plugged into the hand detonator that sent the small electric current that fired the blasting cap and initiated the first explosion. The blast would then travel from tree to tree at 30,000 feet per second, which is pretty much instantaneous to human perceptions.

Having set the charges, the platoon moved back a safe distance and the LT took the detonator out of his pocket. Only now would a  prudent soldier attach the electric cord to the hand detonator (we called it a "clacker" because of the sound it made when you mashed the little lever). For obvious reasons, you must be sure that everyone is under cover before you squeeze the clacker.

The first grunt who befriended me when I was new in the rear was a wild man called "Cherokee." He had been on an earlier mission in the A Shau, and had helped setting charges to blow an LZ, just like we were. He was only half-way back to the safety distance when some dork attached the clacker and blew the charges. Cherokee survived, but his hearing was permanently damaged, and there was a recklessness about him that may have come from having his brain slightly scrambled.

We got down. The LT snapped the clacker. The explosion was huge. The explosion was gorgeous. Every tree was felled in seconds leaving a helicopter-sized hole in the jungle.

It seemed like the slicks showed up almost immediately. We climbed aboard quickly and when we were out of gun range we could finally relax. We were out of the A Shau.

On the flight back, I reflected on my decision to come to the field, and reminded myself - again - that I could have stayed in the rear; I could have remained an REMF.

R.E.M.F.

Rear Escalon Mother Fucker - REMF for short - was the grunt's term of affection for guys in the rear. The term was deserved and recognized by grunts and REMFs alike. Both understood that it took ten men in the rear to support each man in the field. The vast majority of Military Operational Specialties (MOS) were not in the Infantry.

Upon arrival in Vietnam, everyone - including the Infantry - starts in the rear. After a few days of orientation, the grunts report to their combat companies in the field and the REMFs arrive at their duty stations in the rear. For me, however, the most extraordinary turn of fortune fell into my lap. In spite of my Infantry MOS, I became an REMF for the next 6 months.

* * *

It was January 10th, 1970, when I landed in Republic of Vietnam - roughly the middle of a war that began in 1965 and ended in 1975. Our plane arrived at the Ton Son Nut Airport next to Saigon in the early afternoon. The first shock of stepping off the passenger jet that brought us from Guam to Vietnam was overwhelming. First was the heat, and the humidity. I was born in Florida

- where you can drink the air in the summer - and it was never as bad as this. Moving from the modern, air-conditioned interior of the plane onto the exit ramp was like hitting a physical barrier. It stopped me in my tracks. Christmas was only two weeks ago. This was not going to get better.

Then there was the smell. It was a green, damp, jungle smell mixed with the scent of the cooking and the lives of the Vietnamese people. There were few toilets in Vietnam outside of a military base. The fragrance was rounded out with a heavy dose of olive drab from our crisp new uniforms and duffle bags.

The plane was as modern as any commercial Boeing-707 in 1970. On the plane were attractive, American, female flight attendants. Stepping onto the gangway was a change of worlds and cultures that was instantaneous and profoundly disorienting. No wonder they waited several days before they gave us guns

Finally, there was my first sight of the little people wearing pajamas and funny, conical hats. I was shocked to see them within view of the plane. It turned out that many Vietnamese civilians worked for the Americans right on the major bases doing menial tasks such as laundry.

I came to like - maybe love - this people. But I know they went home at night. When they did, they could tell others what was up at the bases. It didn't matter whether it was through their own volition or, just as likely, because people with guns and steel wills asked them nicely.

Those of us bound for the 101st boarded a C-130 the next morning and were flown to the Hue/Phu Bai airport and then trucked to Camp Evans, 24 kilometers northwest of Hue. Here we were to receive our 3 day orientation. This was our opportunity to learn everything we needed to know about Vietnam, the history and customs of its people, and the war.

From the series of presentations delivered to us by no-bullshit non-coms from a stage in a big tent, I remember three things: "Stay Alert and Stay Alive," a good motto in any circumstances; the admonition to remember to pee if you visited a Vietnamese whore (it was supposed to reduce the chances of contracting a venereal disease); and how to say "Get out of here!" and "Halt!" in Vietnamese. Both phrases would prove to be useful.

We were finally issued weapons, taken on a patrol in the local area and stood night perimeter guard in a bunker. It was my first time waiting in the dark for those who ruled the night. By the dawn of the fifth day in Nam, we were Army ready for the field. They loaded us on a truck and drove south to Camp Eagle where we would join our companies as new replacements.

CAMP EAGLE

Camp Eagle was the 101st Airborne's main base camp in Vietnam. It was located near the village of Phu Bai and it was huge. There had to be 5,000 troops stationed there at any one time. It was like a small city where the neighborhoods were the battalions. Surrounding this sprawling city, was a ring of bunkers, watch-towers and to the front of those, the wire. Anything beyond that was considered to be the enemy.

The truck wound its way through the units until it passed a sign emblazoned with "2nd Battalion, 327th Infantry (Airmobile)" and beneath that "No Slack" - our battalion motto. We came to a stop in front of the S-1 (Administration) shack. The dozen or so of us cherries got out of the truck and assembled in a loose formation.

A bored looking staff sergeant came walking down the S-1 shack stairs with a clipboard in his hand. He read off the company assignments for each man. When he got to me he said, "Mobley!?" "Yo!" "Alpha!"

So that was it. I had been assigned to "A" Company. Others in our group were assigned to Bravo, Charlie, Delta and Echo companies - the five Combat companies that made up the No Slack Battalion. When he had assigned everyone to one of the line companies, we picked up our duffle bags and started to move out to our new barracks.

Just then, another Sergeant stepped out of the S-1 shack and, from the top of the wooden stairs, shouted the magic words, "Does anybody here know how to type!?"

It's not true that I almost dislocated my shoulder getting my arm up, but I did see an unexpected opportunity and moved promptly. There was no need to hurry, mine was the only hand raised.

I was told to report to Shorty in the S-4 (Supply) shack. Shorty was literally "short" (his tour was nearly at its end) and they needed a replacement. So my temporary duty was supply clerk instead of infantryman. In this job, I issued equipment to new guys including packs, web gear, canteens, helmets, rifles, etc., and recorded it on the requisite forms with my little typewriter.

I also took back what they still had left when the troops came to check out of country. From the first day, I saw troops both coming and going. I'll never forget the difference in their faces. The fear and trepidation of the Cherries poorly masked by false bravado and the faces (especially the eyes) of the grunts ending their tours, with that long-fixed stare, through and beyond and not really toward anything.

THE LAP OF LUXURY

Life in the rear was pretty much what you would expect at any major Army base. We ate hot meals three times day in a mess hall. We slept on cots in wooden barracks surrounded by sandbags three deep. We took hot showers and wore clean fatigues.

I slept at Alpha Company because I was TDY (temporary duty) to battalion S-4 and was never transferred to Headquarters Company. Most of the time, I was the only soul sleeping in a set of barracks made to hold 100 troops. The other Alpha Company personnel who stayed in the rear were the company sergeant, the company clerk and the company supply sergeant who all had individual rooms. All the rest of the Alpha Company troopers were in the field almost all of the time.

I don't remember the company clerk or the Top sergeant but I'll never forget the supply sergeant: Steve "Bear" Miles. Bear was the right nickname for Steve. He stood around 6' 4" and had arms that seemed to reach to his knees. He was big, he was strong, and he was tough. Being from Massachusetts., he pronounced

Steve "Bear" Miles driving a "Mule"

words like President John Kennedy. A car was a "caw" and Bear was "Beah."

Because I was an S-4 clerk and he was the Alpha Company supply sergeant, I had dealings with Bear several times a week. I confess I was a bit intimidated by Steve. Not only was he physically intimidating, he was a relentless force for supplying his men. Frankly, he had the run of the warehouse since there was no way I was going to tell him no.

The role of a company supply sergeant was critical to the guys in the field. The grunts couldn't come back to a supply location when they needed something. Instead, about once a week, the platoon radio operator (RTO) would call-in a list to the battalion communications center such as: Two pairs of boots, a new pack, 6 two-quart canteens, various ammo, C-Rations for a week, 18 sets of fatigues and so on. The list would be routed to the supply sergeant who would assemble and stage the supplies for the next resupply chopper. Most vitally important, Bear sent us our mail, something more precious than gold.

Unlike a lot of supply sergeants, Bear would frequently ride the resupply bird out and back which he did not have to do. I think perhaps he was a little nostalgic for the bush. Bear was on his third tour of Vietnam and spent the first two years in the field.

The 2/327th Infantry Battalion rear was divided into two parts that were separated by a road running roughly from west to east. On the north side of this road was Headquarters Company, Echo Company, the open-air theater, the battalion chopper pad, the large supply warehouse and the ammo dump.

Lining the other side of the road and forming the north side of a large square was battalion row: the administration, intelligence, operations, communications and supply shacks. The west side of the square was made up of the Alpha and Bravo Companies barracks, the south side was Charlie and Delta Companies, and the east side of the square was the mess hall.

At the open-air theater, we could watch movies at night and see the occasional USO show in the daytime. The mini-skirted girls in the bands were almost all from somewhere nearby - Thailand, Korea, Vietnam. They were appreciated as only a soldier in a war zone can appreciate a pretty girl of any ethnicity. But on the very rare occasions that the performers were American girls, you could feel a tension in the troops. Something akin to barely suppressed frenzy.

Most importantly, there were officer's clubs and EM (enlisted men) clubs. The lower ranks could drink all the beer they could hold and the officers paid 25 cents a shot for the finest scotch. The most abused drug in Vietnam was alcohol.

* * *

It's important to make a distinction between the REMFs and the grunts. The American public's tendency to lump all Vietnam Vets together is not correct. Something like 2.5 million troops served in Vietnam over the course of the war, but the nature of their individual tours was vastly different.

I don't make any judgment on those who served in the rear, especially since I was one. Soldiers had to man the motor pools, the kitchens, the supply process, the administration and a hundred other jobs necessary to prosecute the war. But, there is no way to compare the struggle, suffering and raw danger of the grunts to the comparative comfort and safety of most REMFs - most of the time.

It's also important to note that just sleeping in the rear did not necessarily make you an REMF. Helicopter crews might have slept in the rear but they were not REMFs – especially dust-off crews and close support gunships. While one of our platoons might see action once or twice a month, the air crews served all of the units over a large area and saw much more. Their casualty rates were higher in many cases than most infantry units.

A grunt might be in the rear recovering from wounds and, although they would take a ton of ribbing from their mates when they rejoined the platoon in the field, they were definitely not REMFs.

Doctors, nurses and other medical personnel were not REMFs. Not with what they had to endure treating the endless stream of horribly maimed young men.

* * *

Every couple of months, Alpha Company, my company, would return from the field for a three-day stand-down. They were filthy, stinky, hard young men. You knew instantly if you were looking at a grunt or a REMF - a real soldier or a guy "getting over" (having an easy time). On those rare occasions, I felt distinctly like the comfortable REMF I was - in the company of real warriors.

I was in awe of these guys and a little scared of them, until one of them sort of adopted me. Cherokee (I don't know his real name) decided after my first conversation with him that my handle should be "Poindexter." He liked my word choices and I liked having a friend who was also a real grunt.

Cherokee was the guy who introduced me to the "The Valley of the REMFs." The Valley was a circular depression - probably an old bomb crater - in the center of the battalion square. This is where the Heads gathered on rainless nights to partake in their favorite form of relaxation. They really did occasionally take hits from the barrels of shotguns ("shot-gunning"). The local cannabis was high quality, cheap and easily available to troops in this Cuckoo's nest. For myself and many others, it was one of the few means to sanity. Lots of other guys drank. I did both.

* * *

REMFs, like me, for the most part, just did their everyday, rear echelon jobs. I worked in battalion supply which meant issuing, moving, staging and accounting for the inventory of war. Others worked in administration, intelligence, operations, cooking, repair, communications, and all of the jobs a modern American Army requires.

Enlisted men in the rear also had to do three other duties on rotating bases. The first and worst was KP (Kitchen Patrol). KP meant washing pots and pans all day under the command of tyrannical cooks. It made for a really long day.

The best and shortest rotating detail was the "shit detail." The shit detail was exactly what the name implied. The job consisted of pulling the two-foot wide steel cans (made from the bottoms of fifty-five gallon barrels) from under the holes in the Alpha Company outhouse (ours was a three-holer), pouring diesel oil into the cans and setting it on fire. The final part of the recipe - except for standing upwind - was to stir the mess occasionally with a wooden paddle until only ashes remained). You could knock it off in an hour or two, and you could discretely smoke whatever you wanted since the odor would be undetectable in a cloud of shit smoke and diesel.

Every so often, REMFs also had to stand perimeter-guard at Camp Eagle. This meant getting your weapon and ammo (which you ordinarily didn't carry in the rear) and reporting to your assigned bunker just behind the wire to watch for bad guys all night.

You could be an REMF or a grunt and get tagged for guard duty but, for the most part, regular grunts were spared-perimeter guard and the other details at Eagle because they were grunts. They'd done their sleepless nights for the last 3 months and if they were at Camp Eagle it meant they were on a stand-down. A break. A rest. Besides, REMFs like me needed something almost brave to do to feel more like real soldiers.

GOD AND THE ODD ROCKET

Just because you were in the "rear" did not mean you were out of danger. Vietnam didn't have any front lines. The enemy would harass even such a formidable base as Eagle with rockets, mortars, and even ground attacks on the perimeter by sappers. In May of 1969, a battalion of NVA launched a full-scale sapper attack on Camp Eagle. The 101st lost five men - the enemy lost more than a hundred. The Sappers mostly died in the wire.

Attacks were conducted all over Vietnam against virtually all US and ARVN military positions, particularly the fire bases. The most feared were the Sapper attacks when the enemy tried to penetrate the perimeter undetected. If they made it, they would kill and destroy all they could with TNT satchel charges, RPGs, and small arms.

The indirect-fire weapons – including mortars and the 122 millimeter rockets - were launched from a distance and not always at anything in particular, other than the base itself. The purpose was to create terror - partly through the randomness of the attack - to harass, kill, and most important, create an atmosphere of dread for little risk or cost. And you couldn't hear them coming.

In addition to dying at the hands of the enemy, an REMF like me could become a casualty from acts of the Almighty, or from personal stupidity. I had occasion to try all three – the first two along one very short stretch of road between the place I slept and the place I worked.

Each day, I walked from my barracks to my job at the S-4 shack and back. These spots were only about a hundred yards apart. One day, halfway down the road on my way to my barracks, I was just passing the battalion chopper pad 50 yards to my right. With absolutely no warning, an incoming Katyusha rocket exploded on the center of the helipad. These rockets had a huge warhead filled with TNT and thousands of shrapnel fragments. Fortunately for me, the kill radius for these rockets was about 30 meters - a circle almost one-hundred feet wide. The blast shook me and scared the shit out of me, but I stayed on my feet and didn't get a scratch.

How the NVA managed to hit anything with these unguided monsters remains a mystery to me. The 122 millimeter, 6-foot-long Russian rockets were first used against the Germans in the 1940s as the Soviets drove the Nazis out of Russia and all the way to Berlin. In Vietnam 1970, they still worked really well.

The Russians had used them in the hundreds and thousands, fired from multiple, truck-mounted launch tubes in huge batteries that saturated German positions over large areas. The NVA used them one at a time from homemade launchers, and they were somehow able to hit what they aimed at.

After a prudent interval, I walked over to the impact point. Lying in the middle of the blast area was the rocket nozzle from the base of the Katyusha. It remained because it was a single piece of cast metal weighing 15 pounds and it was in the dead center of the symmetrical explosion. I kept it as an REMF souvenir to prove I had been in a war.

As for divine intervention, a few weeks later, I almost became a casualty a few dozen yards from the spot where I found the rocket nozzle. It was after dark, raining like hell, and I was walking past the battalion ammo dump. The dump was a pit surrounded by an earthen berm and enclosed by a chain-link fence. It held many hundreds of pounds of Infantry ordinance - grenades, C4, mortar rounds, small-arms ammunition, and stuff like that.

I was ten yards away when a most incredible bolt of lightning struck the lightning rod on top of the ammo dump fence. The pillar of electricity was vertical, arrow straight from the sky to the ground, the thickness of a telephone pole, and brighter than I can describe. There was no flash followed by a boom. At 30 feet away, the flash and boom are simultaneous to a human nervous system. I have never heard a louder sound - even in combat. Two thoughts crossed my mind: the Almighty doesn't need a war to take you out, and that was a great place for a lightning rod.

As for an act of stupidity, or at least a serious case of inattention, a month or so after the lightning strike, I nearly managed to break my neck just a little further down the same small section of road.

Throughout Camp Eagle, there were trenches designed to provide cover in the event of an attack. They were about 5 feet deep, 3 feet wide, and of varied length depending on where they were located. Walking toward the battalion outdoor movie screen this particular night, my situational awareness had dropped to zero. My eyes were fixed on the movie screen ahead of me where Liza Minnelli (as Pookie) and Wendell Burton (as Jerry) were staring in the movie "The Sterile Cuckoo."

My wife had just written a letter to me saying this movie reminded her of the two of us. The plot was about mismatched young lovers living through a rocky relationship, until one of them realized they had no future together. I think she was trying to be kind by showing me what I could not see. Her point was that, in some fundamental way, we were simply not suited for one another. Like Jerry and Pokier, we had each acted out of need more than love.

Walking mechanically toward the screen, my complete attention was focused on the movie. The sudden, sickening feeling of falling for a split second ended with my chin slamming down on the far side of the trench I had stepped into. At exactly the same instant, my boots landed at the bottom of the trench. I was stunned and it took a long moment to get over the shock. I spit out the fragments of teeth I had cracked, climbed out of the trench, and went on to see the movie. If the trench had been a few inches deeper (or if I had been a few inches shorter), I would have broken my neck. When I reported to the dentist the next day to show him my cracked teeth, he looked at my mouth and told me I was just fine. The Army didn't do cosmetic dentistry in Vietnam. If I could eat, I was good to go.

BANK SHOT

Four of us REMFs were sitting on top of the perimeter bunker, passing another night on guard detail. At about 0200 hours, we saw them in the distance. One, two, three. The fiery trails from the Katyusha rockets shot into the air from their launchers, two seconds apart and no more than a thousand meters to our front at the one o'clock position. At that distance, the rocket trails looked like Texas bottle rockets. The whooshing sound of the launches followed seconds later: one, two, three. Then, three sonic booms as the Katyushas broke the sound barrier. Up to this point, the four of us sitting on top of the bunker were largely unconcerned. The enemy wouldn't waste a rocket barrage on a perimeter bunker and the sonic booms sounded over our heads as they passed us. We were just spectators.

Then the rockets impacted, 2 seconds apart and 200 yards to our rear, smack dab on a Cobra helicopter pad. Those clever little devils had done it again. Two of the rockets hit the pad squarely and one was just off the edge. One of the burning Cobras parked on the edge of the pad closest to us had its nose pointed directly at our bunker. We were still just watching the show when the landing skid on that Cobra burned through. The attack helicopter fell more than 30 degrees and the pod on the right-hand side of the Cobra began to fire its rockets. The first rocket went over our heads and exploded to our front. The second rocket impacted 50 meters to our rear, between our bunker and the Cobra. Suddenly, we stopped being spectators.

As Murphy's Law requires, the third rocket was aimed straight for the middle of our bunker. We saw it take flight from the gunship and the four of us dove to the trenches that lay on either side of the bunker. The three other guys jumped to the right and I dove to the left. I took one step and executed a racing dive I learned on the swim team at Sanger High. A racing drive requires you to launch horizontally in a long, flat dive designed for maximum distance. If a racing dive doesn't hurt when you hit the water, you didn't do it right. I was still in the air when the third rocket struck our bunker dead-center. If we hadn't jumped off in that last second, we all would have been casualties.

Return artillery fire was pointless. The NVA gunners were gone from their launching positions before their rockets landed. Three, twelve-million dollar Cobras, were destroyed for the price of three Katyusha rockets donated for free to the NVA by the Russians and Chinese. Even though the rockets themselves were free, our enemy's human cost to carry them from the ports of North Vietnam, down the Ho Chi Minh trail, through the A Shau Valley, and, finally, south-east of Camp Eagle where they set them up and launched them at the chopper pad.

A GI from another bunker took a picture of the four of us surrounding the rocket crater, flashing the peace sign, and smiling like a bunch of idiots. The NVA almost got us with a bank shot.

THE LIBRARY

One day, I found out there was a library at the 101st Division Headquarters (HQ) at Camp Eagle. At my first opportunity, I went to find it.

The library was housed in a double-wide trailer in the HQ compound. As I opened the door and walked in, I was rendered speechless. *The room was air-conditioned!* It was the first cool, dehumidified air I had breathed since getting off the plane months before. I couldn't speak for several moments. Then, I turned to the E-6 standing behind the counter. He was right out of a recruiting poster - tall, blond, fit - looking good with his starched fatigues and polished boots. I was finally able to talk and blurted out, "You work here?" He just grinned and nodded. Like I said before, not all tours were the same.

To my amazement, the room looked like a library. There was modern furniture, carpet, shelves of books, and *no* windows to let the Nam in. I found a chair, sat back, closed my eyes, and suddenly I was home. It was quite a while before I opened my eyes.

At first, I just enjoyed breathing the wonderful, cool air. With my eyes shut, I could have been in any air conditioned room back in the World. But slowly, gradually, a pain started deep in my chest. Now, each new breath became a memory of home that clashed with the truth of where I was. After a while, I couldn't stand it any longer.

Since it was a library and I felt guilty for sitting in the coolness for so long, I finally got up and went to the bookshelves. As luck would have it, the first collection I saw was a shelf of National Geographic editions. One of these contained a fold-out star chart of the whole sky. As I looked at the chart, a sudden realization struck me. Astronomy has been a hobby of mine since I was 12, but my viewing had always been limited to those features visible from Fresno, California at 36 degrees north latitude. Camp Eagle - just south of Hue - was at 17 degrees north latitude. As the star chart showed, from there I could see the Southern constellations for the first time.

I asked the clerk if I could have the star chart. He said sure. I stuck it in my pocket and left. I never went back to the library. I couldn't stand the ache.

ASTRONOMY ON THE PERIMTER

The first perimeter guard I drew after I found the star chart at the library was a jet-black, moonless night. I volunteered to man one of the watch towers. These towers were spaced about every fourth fighting bunker. They were 40 feet tall and getting up one meant climbing an external wooden ladder, which scared the hell out of me. The towers were exposed and unfortified. You did not fight from the towers. They were only for spotting the enemy and, if you did, you got the hell down in a hurry and made your way to a bunker. This lookout post was usually not a favorite position for anyone.

However, this night, I had a plan. These the towers were equipped with starlight scopes - great, big, starlight scopes. Mounted on a tripod roughly 8 inches wide at the lens end and about 18 inches long tapering to the eyepiece, these  bulky early night vision devices could intensify the available light into a ghostly green image that allowed you to see the enemy coming.

To get to the scope, you had to climb an additional ladder to the roof of the tower. There was no guardrail on top of this tower - just a flat wooden floor, and sudden death if you stepped off. Even staying away from the edge, I felt that funny feeling in my stomach you get on high places. But I had a mission - two actually.

First was my duty to look for bad guys. I scanned the rolling hills west of Camp Eagle for a long time. There was no movement. I seized my opportunity.

A starlight scope works on the principal of a tiny, square chip called a "charge-coupled device (CCD)." You can think of it as grid (like a checkerboard) of tiny light detectors so sensitive, each one of the little squares can sense a single photon. These are all linked together electronically, and their tiny signal announces the arrival of the photons and is boosted many times to a visible image. When you look at terrain, even if there is only starlight, you can see the landscape and anything in it.

When you point the starlight scope directly at the sky or any faint light source - a star or a galaxy - the object shines with a beautiful, intense, green radiance that is much more than the naked eye can see. As I pointed the starlight scope straight up, where I had seen hundreds of stars I now saw many thousand - the skies over Vietnam exploded with brilliance. It took my breath away.

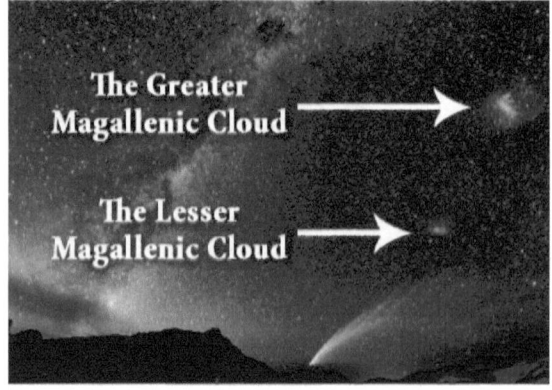

I saw the breathtaking constellation called The Crux - the Southern Cross - the brightest and most beautiful of the Southern constellations. I saw the Clouds of Magellan.

These fuzzy naked eye objects were first recorded by the adventurous Spaniard, Ferdinand Magellan, on his historic voyage to complete the first circumnavigation of the Earth in 1522. In modern times, they are called "The Greater Magellanic Cloud" and "The Lesser Magellanic Cloud". We now know that these "clouds" are complete galaxies in their own right and are the closest galactic neighbors to our own Milky Way.

That night I saw many other objects in the sky of South-East Asia that cannot be seen from the San Joaquin Valley of Central California. Because of being drafted into Vietnam, I had this opportunity, a few minutes of transcendent beauty on a battle line.

UNFRIENDLY FIRE

It was 12 days before Christmas when the explosion detonated in the middle of the Enlisted Men's (EM) club in the Eagle rear. At first, everybody thought it was incoming. It would not be long before the horrible truth became clear. A frag had been thrown into this room full of soldiers by another soldier. This was the other way to die in the rear - at the hands of another G.I.

I was in the field near FSB Birmingham that day, but there were 3 Alpha Company grunts in the club that night. Sgt. Mike Harris had been my squad leader and was just days away from going home. He was sitting at the bar in the EM club when the explosion detonated in the center of the room. Like any combat grunt, his reflex was to find cover. He dove over the bar while his brain tried to locate the danger. It would be over an hour before he noticed his pant leg was soaked with blood from the shrapnel embedded in his shin.

PFC Ray Sellers was seated near the small stage among a group of grunts from Illinois. They were singing "Chicago - What a Wonderful Town" in honor of one of their buddies about leave Vietnam to return to the Windy City. He was blown off his chair and knocked unconscious, but he thinks he was the only soldier among the three dozen or so in the club who did not receive any external wounds. Ray thinks the troops between him and the blast took the shrapnel. I met Ray soon after near firebase Birmingham when he joined 1st Platoon in the field. He was the platoon's newest replacement but he didn't say a single word to me about the fragging that had almost killed him days earlier.

Don Lance remembers the room going black when the generator was knocked out. Then the moans and cries filled the rom. Don crawled towards the door which was lit by the full moon outside. He still thought it was incoming and, once outside, jumped into the trench next to the club. It was half full of water. Others who could move crawled over each other to get outside and fell into it.

When it became clear that it was not incoming, Don climbed out of the fighting trench. He remembers seeing the profile of a GI backlit by the moon who was missing his nose. Ray went through training with a kid from Chicago who "had his face blown of." Other casualties ranged from Mike's shin to critical. I don't know if any of those died.

* * *

At this point in the war, the tension, the collapse of morale, the lack of discipline, and the racial animosity in the rear had become palpable. Everyone knew the war was lost and our lives were on the line for nothing.

The growing racial tension that poisoned the REMF atmosphere was never an issue for the grunts in the field. It just didn't happen. You had to rely on your platoon mates, and racial problems just didn't exist in the bush.

The man who threw the frag was almost certainly an REMF with a grudge. In the madness of this stage of the war, the fratricide that the soldier committed on his brothers was almost mundane. It was clearly an act of insanity made unusual only by the target he chose.

"Fragging" - the act of attacking officers that some enlisted men thought had put them in unnecessary danger or who *might* put them in danger - had increased so much that it affected command decisions. There were lieutenants and captains who avoided actions - even disobeying direct orders - out of a sense of self-preservation. Some had bounties put on their heads. This influenced their behavior.

THE BROKEN PEACE SIGN

The cook and I were returning from a chow run to one of our platoons. I was driving the ¾ ton truck and the cook was riding shotgun. Occasionally, when the grunts got out of the bush and close to the highway, our battalion would send a truck with a hot meal. The meals were cooked in the rear and put into Mermite containers that were incredibly well insulated. The grunts got hot food even hours after it was cooked.

These little missions got me out of the rear and let me see the real Vietnam. I volunteered for them at every opportunity. The grunts were always grateful for a break from C rations and it made us feel good to bring them good food. The cooks in the battalion rear prepared nutritious, tasty meals, in spite of the institutional requirement that all Army cooks

Xmas Dinner, 3rd Platoon

gripe incessantly.

On our return, we were passing a small hamlet a few miles south of Eagle when I spotted a little road-side stand. It was made of scrap wood cobbled together and was maybe 6 feet wide. On the stand hung various and sundry objects that might interest a GI. My attention was drawn by a guitar hanging on one side and I pulled over.

The guitar was built locally. I didn't expect much but I picked it up and plucked the tinny metal strings. I ran the scale up the neck, and to my surprise, it fretted true.

"How much?" I asked the little Vietnamese woman. "Five dolla," she replied.

I was supposed to say 2 dollars and she was supposed to say 4 after which we would settle at 3 but I just gave her the 5 bucks. I had a real guitar to play.

I was turning to leave when something hanging from the wooden crossbeam that framed the top of the tiny stand caught my eye. It was a golden, broken, peace pendant - shining brightly and glinting occasionally as it turned slowly on the end of a silver chain.

The pendant wasn't actually "broken." It was purposely designed with a gap in the outer border where the right leg of the upside-down trident of the peace sign met the edge, to represent a "broken peace." It symbolized my crazy journey to war perfectly.

SCHOOL LEARNIN

Harry Truman was president when I was born in 1948. He dropped the Bomb and won the war, but my first memory of a president was Dwight David Eisenhower. He had been "Supreme Commander of Allied Forces in Europe" and may have been the first president for whom the title "President of the United States" was a demotion. My Dad liked Ike so I liked Ike, as I argued to my four-square opponents at Roeding Elementary School in Fresno, California when I was 6. Ike was elected in 1952 and re-elected in 1956.

On March 29th, 1953, my family and I watched the light of an atomic bomb blast in the east from the front yard of our small home in Fresno. Even at 5 years old, seeing a nuclear flash backlight the crest of the Sierra Nevada Mountains told me this was something very big. The Nevada Test Site was over 200 miles away.

* * *

My father served as a signalman aboard the heavy cruiser USS Minneapolis in the Battle of Leyte Gulf during WWII - the largest engagement in the history of naval warfare. He was completely nonpartisan and voted for John Kennedy over Richard Nixon in 1960. As a twelve-year-old, I thought President Kennedy was the greatest person in the world. In those first years of his presidency, you could practically smell the hope in the air. Then, the Cuban Missile Crisis scared us all to death in late 1962. The world didn't seem so hopeful anymore.

On the day of my 15th birthday, June 11, 1963, a Buddhist monk named Thích Quảng Đức, deliberately and with the help of his friends, set himself ablaze at a busy intersection in Saigon. He did

this to protest the oppression of Buddhists by the Catholic president of South Vietnam, Ngo Dinh Diem. President Kennedy said, "No news picture in history has generated so much emotion around the world as that one." [xi] At Sanger High, I was in my International Relations class when I first read the story. It was my first awareness that a place called Vietnam existed.

President Kennedy insisted that Diem cease his crackdown on the Buddhists. Diem ignored him. Washington began to distance itself from his regime. Five months later, on November 2, 1963, Diem was shot dead in the back of a van as his brother was knifed to death beside him. This military coup by South Vietnamese officers was conducted with the collusion and approval of the CIA, the American ambassador to Vietnam, high ranking American military officers and some in and near the White House. The Secretary of Defense, Robert McNamara, said,

"When the President received the news, he literally blanched. I had never seen him so moved... Kennedy was personally shaken by the event. The murder 'bothered him as a moral and religious mat-

ter . . . shook his confidence . . . in the kind of advice he was getting about South Vietnam." [xv]

Twenty days after that, John Kennedy was shot dead in Dallas, Texas. America's future, and my future, were changed forever.

As he flew back to Washington, Lyndon Baines Johnson was sworn in as President of the United States with Kennedy's wife, Jacquie, standing at his side, her dress stained with the blood of her husband. The blood of millions would follow in the war Johnson was about to start.

By the time I entered Fresno State College in the fall of 1966, I was 18 and Vietnam had flared into a full-fledged American ground war. The draft stuck terror in the hearts of millions of young men who had not volunteered. The privileged - like me - got student deferments. Our draft cards were stamped "2-S" and we were safe as long as we stayed in college. Those without privilege were rated "1-A (available for the draft). Conscripts were picked randomly by a "Selective Service System" through means of a "lottery."

"Selective service" sounds much nicer than "involuntary conscription." The draft seemed to me to be the moral equivalent of "Shanghaiing." The term was coined in the mid-19th century, and referred to the practice of commercial vessels who would  fill shortages in their ship's crews by knocking drunks on the head and dragging them aboard ship. When they woke, they were at sea, under the authority of the Captain, and mutiny was a capital offense. They served.

The draft picked one and skipped another, kind of like a tornado and just as lethal. For those selected, there were no good options. Some rushed to get married and have children. Others left the country, mostly for Canada. Doctors helped some with fake diagnosis. There were those desperate enough to mutilate their own bodies. A very few went to jail on principle. The majority resigned themselves to their fate and prayed with their families that they would return.

RESISTANCE

The voice of Joan Baez soared over the crowd with crystalline clarity. She was singing a Bob Dylan song as much from her heart as her mouth.

> *"How many times can a man turn his head and pretend that he just doesn't see?"* [xii]

Her voice and the song penetrated my soul and convicted me. I could see - I had been able to for a long time - and I was pretending.

It was a gentle spring night and the audience was seated on the grass of the amphitheater at Fresno State College. I was up-close, right in front of the stage, watching one of my favorite artists speak against the war in Vietnam. She was accompanied by her husband, David Harris, who had founded a movement called "The Resistance." David was a Fresno native and the former student body president of Stanford University. His mission was to oppose the Selective Service System and the Vietnam War using nonviolent, civil disobedience. The strategy was simple. If enough young men refused to cooperate with the draft, they could break the apparatus that fed the war.

Even if Harris' tactic failed, the resistors would still have the moral satisfaction of not participating in a war they considered immoral. They just had to be willing to go to the federal penitentiary at Leavenworth, Kansas to preserve their principals. I bought it.

When I returned my first draft card in a small ceremony at Fresno State in April of 1968, along with 12 other resistors, we put them in an envelope addressed to General Hershey who headed the draft system. The envelope was taken by a local pastor and placed into a campus mailbox.

Then, a few of us spoke. I said to the small crowd:

"It is inconceivable to me that any man, any group of men, or any nation can demand such unquestioning, such unthinking obedience of an individual that they can require him, by law, to participate in the organized mass slaughter of his fellow man regardless of his personal beliefs about the morality of the act he is called on to perform. . . . That such a state of affairs can exist in a supposedly democratic nation is unbelievable."

Of course, a replacement card with the "2-S" changed to "1-A" arrived shortly thereafter. After I sent that one back too, I received my first induction notice.

A dozen or so supporters stood outside the Fresno Induction Center as I formally refused induction. After a second refusal, the FBI climbed all over my life and, inevitably, I was indicted by a Federal Grand Jury. The Federal District Judge at the time, M. D. Crocker, had a simple formula. The army will give you two, I'll give you three.

My girlfriend left me, my studies tanked, and I found myself in the office of the chairman of the psychology department dejectedly asking what I should do. By the end of our conversation, I folded. He called the US Attorney on the spot and cut a deal. I go to Vietnam and they drop charges. What a deal. I think I would have felt better if they had just knocked me on the head and thrown my unconscious body on a boat.

* * *

A year had passed and now I was standing in front of a roadside souvenir stand in a small hamlet in Vietnam buying a broken peace sign to wear around my neck. It was my personal Albatross. I also had a serviceable guitar.

Back in the rear, I wrote a little song with that guitar. The first verse goes:

"Well I found out something just the other day I wanna tell you.
I really found out that there's really not nothing much true.
I found out I didn't know anything I thought I knew.
And, my friend neither do you."

A short time after I wrote that classic, they asked for a volunteer to go to Fire Support Base Tomahawk as a mule driver. On my first night on T-Hawk, the attack by the 71B Sapper Company of the 4th NVA Regiment changed everything. Whatever vestige of distance

I held in my mind was erased the instant I was blasted out of my bunk by that RPG.

A CALL FROM MARS

"Is he there now?" I asked my wife over the radio handset. "Yes," she replied after a long moment. The troops standing around me in the small waiting area grimaced and averted their eyes. A "Dear John" letter was common in Vietnam, but an open phone call that other soldiers could hear revealing that your wife was - at that moment - in bed with another man, was a cut above.

Right after I returned to the rear after the sapper attack on T-Hawk, I went to the M. A. R. S. (Military Amateur Relay Service) hooch to make a call home. The battle and the bodies were still in my head. I needed to talk to someone back in the World. My bad timing was not her fault.

* * *

My wife and I met in the summer of '66 when I was 18 and she was 16. She was beautiful and whip smart. We lived together in our tiny one-room Hobbit Hole a few blocks from Fresno State in '67 and '68. She was with me at the Fresno Induction Center the first time I officially refused induction in front of the unit commander. By complete chance, she ran into an old boyfriend who had just returned from Vietnam. He was still in uniform and happened to be stationed at the induction center for his last duty station. Talk about luck. The spark between them was still there and my future looked decidedly dim. He would become my "Jodie."

In fairness to my once and future wife, there was no deceit. I think I began falling in love with her just about the same time she was falling out of love with me. The FBI started knocking at my door and interviewing everybody I had ever known. She moved out to live with a girlfriend, and that was truly the end of our relationship.

When I was a month away from Vietnam, I professed my love and made her an offer. Marry me (again), get the monthly spousal stipend the Army provided, become the beneficiary of the small life-insurance policy the government would pay in the event of my death, and, as she wished, continue or terminate the marriage on my return. I had a hard time letting go of my first love and I still had hope. She took the deal. We were married in Carson City, Nevada. There was no honeymoon.

After the "Dear Jim" phone call, I walked back to Alpha Company blinded by tears. I sat down on a cot, in a row of cots, in a completely empty barracks. Alone, wallowing in my misery and self-pity, something quite strange happened.

There are no suitable words to tell it, but it seemed as though the Almighty reached down his hand, tore back the tin roof on the barracks, cast a bolt of lightning through my soul, froze me in place, and asked me a question. The question was *"where is your pain coming from?"*

I actually turned to look around the large room. Not only were there no human beings, there was also no evil presence poking me in the ribs with a pitchfork. I really was _totally_ alone. My suffering _had_ to come from within myself. The flash of insight was startling.

"*Who are you?*" was the next question. I took inventory and found I was near the pinnacle of the pyramid of humanity and I should stop whining. I was half an inch short of six feet tall, I had good friends, my health was excellent, I would finish my education, and my future prospects were bright.

The list went on. By the end, the anguish of losing my first love gently receded as if you had slowly closed the door to a home you were leaving for the last time. I stood up in the empty barracks and strode purposefully out the door. I was headed for Echo Company. I had made a decision.

FUCK IT

I could not look the grunts in the face any longer and sit on my ass in the rear while they were fighting a war for me. Not after Tomahawk. They were grunts and everybody else wasn't. They humped hard and faced grave danger. I was ashamed to be an REMF who slept on a cot and ate in a mess-hall. You did your office job and could have a beer at night and see a movie. There were real latrines and you could take a shower every day. It wasn't fair. I decided to go to the field.

* * *

I believe there are certain qualities in Americans that makes them among the best warriors on Earth. You don't even have to train us very much. We are trained by the age of eight through our uniquely-American combat role playing as children. For the most part, you just have to give us weapons and point us at an enemy. In every case, that enemy is going to have a problem.

We Americans think on our feet and we seem to have a special aptitude and affinity for blowing things up and killing people. Perhaps the one redeeming outcome of the Vietnam War was that we proved that we were bold enough and crazy enough to try to do what we did. Every nation on earth must take it into consideration that America can go stark raving nuts and we are not the kind of people you want to piss off.

There is also, I believe, an impulse within men, forged by our culture, our movies, our books and our play, that compels us to want to "prove ourselves" in battle. A good dose of testosterone rounds out the formula. I believe most men ask themselves the question, "how would I act in combat." I also believe that, if the truth be known, there is a niggling uneasiness - and perhaps shame - in those who have avoided military service through chance or purpose. Shakespeare captured this idea perfectly when he wrote, "... *And gentlemen ... now a-bed, Shall think themselves accursed they were not here, and* **hold their manhood's cheap** [my emphasis]."

My generation was not only raised on compelling movies about war, we were surrounded by the real life soldiers, sailors and airmen - our fathers - who won WWII through their bravery, dedication, and sacrifice. My generation saw the honor and the glory of these men, things they themselves dismissed. We embraced the stories and the myths that surrounded them and we wanted it for ourselves. Some express this desire through daydreams and exciting scenarios woven with other arm-chair warriors over a six-pack. A *very* few others, do the real deal, and know the terrible answer to the question of how they would act. And I felt I was *missing my war!*

* * *

I headed for Echo Company because that was where the mortar platoon was headquartered. At the beginning of AIT at Ford Ord, California, a few of us trainees were assigned to mortars. During mortar training, we were enthralled by tales from the drill sergeants and cadre who had just returned from Vietnam. These battle hardened authorities were fond of telling us how lucky we mortar-men were. Not only were we unlikely to hump - being stationed at a fixed location - but, we were told, there would be ample opportunity for commerce and collaboration with the local civilians. You could obtain extra-curricular supplies of all sorts and the tales of hooch-mates who took care of the cleaning, the washing and oh so much more made us almost eager to get there.

I really didn't want to hump. When we took the final gunner's exam in AIT, I got 191 points out of a possible 191 points. On graduation day, they gave me a cute little trophy with a plate naming me the outstanding trainee in mortars for my AIT brigade.

So, as I marched into the Echo Company area, I figured the Army would want to leverage their investment in my training. The friendly mortar platoon leader at Echo Company listened to my pitch and said sure, he'd take me, but I would have to clear it with the battalion XO.

The XO listened impatiently as I made my request explaining my reasons and training. He barely paused before saying no. They didn't need any mortar men but they did still need a typist/driver/gopher in supply. As an infantryman, I had one more card to play - one I knew he couldn't refuse. I said, "Fuck it! Send me to the field!"

I stepped off the resupply helicopter and joined 1st platoon in the field less than 24 hours later.

FIELD TRIP

FOOT IN MOUTH DISEASE

When the Slick landed at 1st Platoon's day pause, I stepped off the chopper and directly onto my tongue. To this day, I can't fathom how those words spilled out of my mouth except for the extreme nervousness of being the Fucking New Guy (FNG). I found the platoon leader and introduced myself as his new replacement. Then, my cherry ass blurted out something like; "Do all these guys have their shit together?" or maybe it was "I hope all these guys have their shit together." Whatever I said, it was the kind of remark that might have been appropriate from a field-grade officer like a general or coronel but not by the newest cheery in the platoon. I probably could not have said anything more stupid.

The LT stared back at me - stared way through me - and, after a minute, slowly said in quiet, even tones that made it worse. "All of these men have served with me in combat." I knew I had insulted the lieutenant and the whole platoon as soon as the words were out of my mouth. I wanted them back but it was too late. It would take me months to live them down.

I immediately picked up a stern attitude from the NCOs and I'm pretty sure the LT gave them a heads-up about the new cherry. There was one trooper named Ed Schlappi who sort of took me under his wing that first day and showed me the essential ropes of field life. He taught me how to make a stove out of an empty C-ration can, the importance of light and noise discipline at night, and to watch out for light-fingered locals when re-supplying in the lowlands. Ed was one of the most even-tempered guys I've ever met. On what was otherwise a pretty shitty start to my field life, he offered friendship that made everything a little easier.

TOM

What I didn't know the day I joined the platoon - and what made my remark so much worse - was that 1st platoon had lost a squad leader, Sgt. Tom Catlin, just days before. The shock to their guts was still as raw as it could be. But grunts did not show the emotion or even talk about such things.

Later, I would learn Sergeant Catlin had been critically wounded by a booby trap. They were in deep bush under heavy canopy and twilight was falling. At the instant of the explosion, everyone sprang into action. Tom was moved back to the CP for first aid while most of the platoon assumed a high alert defensive posture around the perimeter. Any enemy in the area now knew exactly where they were.

Sgt. Roger Roy and Sgt. Mike Harris immediately began CPR while Doc and the LT fought desperately to stop the bleeding from Tom's leg. His injuries were severe and they had only limited success. Tom was slipping away in spite of their best efforts. Blast trauma, shrapnel wounds, shock and the critical damage to his leg caused him to gradually lose consciousness.

Sgt. Bill Beasley was the squad leader who knew Tom the best. They had gone through training together and arrived in the Nam just thirty-five days earlier. They were friends before they got to

1st Platoon. The last words Tom spoke before losing consciousness were a call out for his friend Bill.

They kept up CPR for over an hour until the helicopter arrived. At first, the helicopter couldn't find them. This was triple-canopy jungle and it was dark. No light could reach from the floor to the sky. The pilot knew he was close to the platoon because he was in radio contact and the platoon could hear the helicopter. But the helicopter crew couldn't see them. Ordinary signaling devices such as smoke or lights were useless.

hat's when Barney Barnes, the platoon RTO, grabbed a strobe light and began climbing a tall tree closest to Tom. Barehanded and unarmed, he climbed to the very top of the tree, turned on the strobe light, and held it up over his head as high as he could. The helicopter pilot guided on the light until the bird was finally able hover over the platoon. Strangely, Barney does not remember doing this. However, I talked to 5 other members of 1st platoon who saw him do it

Since there was absolutely no place to land, this had to be a combat extraction using a litter lowered though the trees on a cable. The basket was lowered to the ground and Tom's comrades placed him on the litter. Only then did they cease the CPR. He was immediately hoisted up to the waiting medics on the dust-off crew and they headed at top speed to the 95th Evacuation Hospital at Da Nang - about 15 air minutes away.

Sgt. Roger Roy was monitoring the radio when the transmission came in 15 minutes later. "Delta Oscar Alpha" (DOA) said the voice from Da Nang.

SKY PILOT

A cold shock of fear rushed up my spine when my situation hit me. I was in the center of a landing zone, with a large cache of food and ammunition, and I was alone. It was first time I found myself in a totally exposed position, and the feeling shook me to my bones. Real or imagined, I could feel unfriendly eyes. My cherry blood turned cold.

I had been in-country for over six months, and I had been in combat during the sapper attack on Tomahawk, but I was as green in the field as a newborn. I'd gotten off on the wrong foot with the platoon leadership and I felt the distance acutely. I would probably have had a better chance of staying out of trouble if communication had been better. Anyway, that's my excuse for getting into this situation in the first place.

It started at the end of the Chaplain's service. Occasionally, these "Sky Pilots" would visit a combat platoon in the field for religious ministration. About half the guys attended the service and the rest went about their business. I hung back on the edge of the service but didn't participate. I couldn't tell you what the sermon was about, but I was impressed that these unarmed pastors, priests, rabbis or whatever would come out to a combat zone to deliver non-sectarian services for the spiritual wellbeing of the troops. That's another kind of bravery. After the completion of his religious service, he gathered up his stuff and we contacted the inbound slick on the radio.

I had been assigned as the squad RTO - the guy with the radio. My squad leader told me to accompany the Chaplain back to the landing zone and bring in the chopper. *I'm sure he said the rest of the squad would be right behind me.*

The pastor and I walked the couple of hundred yards to the LZ and I contacted the inbound pilot. "Lancer 27, this is King 6 X-ray"

"King 6 X-ray, pop smoke" the pilot instructed.

I took out one of the smoke grenades we all carried, tossed a green one into the center of the landing zone and radioed, "Lancer 27, smoke out."

"Confirm green smoke" the pilot radioed when he saw it.

"Green smoke confirmed," I replied.

This identification protocol was necessary because the enemy would sometimes pop their own smoke in an attempt to misdirect a helicopter into an ambush. We had green, blue, red, purple, yellow, white and orange which we picked at random. This decreased the odds the enemy would guess the correct color.

The pilot executed a perfect landing in the center of the LZ- touching down ever so lightly as only a helicopter can. They were carrying a week's worth of food for twenty men plus ammo and a replacement M60 machine gun.

The helicopter crew handed me and the Chaplain the cases from the chopper and we stacked them on the ground. These helicopter crews ferried us around, brought us our supplies, and, most importantly, would attempt to come through almost anything to retrieve our wounded. They rate at the top of the bravery list and they paid dearly for their courage during the entire Vietnam War.

There is nothing more dangerous to a UH-1 Delta helicopter

than flying low and slow, or worse, sitting on the ground. These aircraft were not armored and small arms could kill their crew or take down the aircraft.

It took maybe two minutes to unload the supplies. The Chaplain said goodbye and climbed into the bird. They took off the instant the Chaplain was seated. I waved goodbye and, as they disappeared into the sky, the situation suddenly dawned on me. I was standing in the middle of an LZ - surrounded by jungle - all by myself - next to a fair sized stack of cases containing food, ammunition and a brand new M60 machine gun. A lightly armed Boy Scout troop could have taken me out and seized that cache. I think if I had looked in a mirror I would have been white.

I got on the radio and called back to the platoon. I can't remember what I said but it's fair to say I expressed concern regarding my situation. Then, while I waited, I loaded a belt of ammo into the M60. It was far and away the best firepower I had. I stacked the C-Ration cases into a very short wall and got behind them to give me some cover in the bare LZ.

After a long five or ten minutes, the squad showed up moving quickly. To say the least, I was relieved. "How come you didn't hold the chopper!" someone barked. Now I was embarrassed. *I was supposed to hold the chopper?* Even as a Cherry, that didn't sound right. *You don't hold a helicopter on the ground for the convenience of a platoon.* When we got back to the platoon with the supplies, they took away my radio.

I do not know what really happened. Maybe I was setup. Maybe someone just made a mistake. Still, I knew I was already on the platoon shit list so I said nothing. For the next couple of months, I just kept my mouth shut and quietly did my job. Gradually, I think I gained respect from the most of the platoon leadership and healed the damage from my poor start.

Months later, I was sitting on a cot in a large tent in the No Slack rear during a stand down when the LT came over to say goodbye. He was leaving 1st Platoon for his next assignment. As I stood to shake his hand, he said "you've been a good soldier Mobley." I said "thank you, Sir." I felt a little like I had been forgiven.

CAMPING OUT

Regardless of our location - mountains or lowlands - life in the field sucked. The heat and humidity were incredible. When we moved, we carried a huge weight on our backs. Combined with the heat it was almost unbearable. Many of us wore a towel around our necks, in spite of the heat, in order to soak up the sweat constantly pouring from our faces. Heat exhaustion was not uncommon. I came close to dropping several times in eight months.

Then there was the goddamned rain. In the 101st AO of Thua Thien and Quang Tri provinces, it rains 118 inches per year in the flatlands and more in the mountains. Monsoon season runs from June through September, but even in the "dry" season we were always wet - soaked by sweat if not by rain. Moving anywhere meant constantly crossing streams or canals. The only good news was that the temperature - even in the winter - didn't drop below the 60's.

During any average three months, we could expect to get a few days on firebases securing the perimeters, and we would get a stand-down at Camp Eagle for maybe 3 days in 90. The rest of the time we lived in the field for weeks and months that seemed endless. We owned the lowlands. The enemy owned the mountains.

At night, our bed was the ground, our ceiling was the sky. Sleeping on the ground is not, in and of itself, a problem. If you are tired enough, you can sleep almost anywhere. During the night, half of the platoon had to be awake at any given time to watch out for bad guys.

I pulled my guard starting with deep slugs of "ambush coffee." That was my name for the instant coffee in C-rations. Almost nobody else in the platoon would drink this stuff because it was really lousy coffee. The upside was that it contained an extra strong dose of caffeine. After a resupply, I gathered the individual packets of coffee from my platoon mates who weren't going to use them. Just before it got dark, I poured *nine* of the packets into a canteen of water, shook it vigorously and put it back in my canteen pouch for later. When I was roused for my turn on watch, the first thing I did was to drink a third of the canteen - three strong cups of coffee in 10 seconds. It worked. Caffeine mixed with fear kept me alert.

The food wasn't bad if you weren't too picky. C-rations are nutritious and some are tasty. Along with the canned food, the packages came with cigarettes, salt, sugar, chewing gum, matches, toilet paper, instant coffee, and heat tabs (solid compressed cooking fuel). If you ran out of heat tabs, you could always use a piece of C-4,

Re-supply "Kick-Out"

which burned just fine without exploding. After a while, C-rations could become a bit boring. GI's were always trying new combinations and inventing new ways to spice them up. A guy who received a bottle of Tabasco sauce from home became an instant hero.

When our re-supply birds couldn't land because we were in deep bush with no LZ, they just kicked the C-ration cartons out the bird and they fell - undamaged - to the ground. They were packaged in two layers of really tough cardboard. We used the thick outer cardboard sleeve to cover our rucksack frames so the cross bars didn't dig into our backs.  They were so strong, the Vietnamese refugees used them to build the walls of their shelters.

Taking a shit in the boonies always felt dangerous to me. You took an entrenching tool (a small, folding shovel), found a bush to shield your privacy, dug a hole, squatted over it, and did your business. It always felt like an exposed situation – it's a difficult posture to fight from – and I nervously scanned the immediate area keeping my M16 at the ready. You didn't linger and read a magazine like you could in the rear.

One life form we could have done without was the leeches - lots and lots of leeches. Nobody likes to sleep with leeches. These little parasites are - by definition - creepy. And they were everywhere. The land leeches moved about like a short inchworm. First they extended their stretchy little bloodsucking bodies and grabbed onto the ground with the sucker end. Then they let loose of their other end and brought it forward to meet the front. Repeat until a warm blooded animal - preferably a grunt - is found.

You couldn't feel them when they were feeding because they had surgically sharp little teeth shaped in a circle and they secreted a local anesthetic to numb the site. When they were full of your blood and swollen to the size of a grape, they would let go and fall off.

If you discovered them before they were full and dropped from your body, there were two methods to get them to let go. You could touch them with the burning end of a cigarette. Or much better, you could drop bug juice on them. "Bug Juice" was a powerful Army insect repellant which worked against all biting bugs and kept the little bastards away. As a leech killer, however, it was truly at its greatest glory. One small drop on a feeding leech and it disgorged the blood it had already sucked in, spilling it on your body. Then it and bubbled and writhed like you had poured sulfuric acid on it as it fell to the ground. The bug juice - 100 percent DEET (diethyltoluamide) was developed by the Army after the jungle fighting of WWII caused so many casualties from malaria and other insect-borne illnesses. It was oily and smelly, but after twenty-four hours in the field you stopped noticing.

I applied it liberally to any exposed skin and any opening a leech could exploit. If you had any brains, you kept your fatigue trousers tucked firmly into you boots. Personally, I didn't have much trouble with leaches, but apparently some of us taste better than others. I recall Sgt. McCubbins being so afflicted he would use a whole bottle of bug juice at once to squirt a ring around his sleeping position to keep them away at night.

River leeches were worse, though less frequent, since you need to walk though water to encounter them. They were much longer, swam in all the streams, and we frequently had to ford those streams. It was possible to keep them off your legs with well-sealed trousers but you could not keep them off your body with the loose fitting jungle fatigue shirts. After water crossing, we stripped down and did a buddy check on our backs to find the leeches you could not see or feel yourself. Worst of all was finding them attached to your private parts.

In the field, I had to completely change the way I slept. Before Nam, I always put my glasses on the nightstand and I shifted through the night as everyone does. Once I was in the field, this was no longer possible. The first night I slept in the field, I took off my glasses and placed them inside my steel pot to keep them safe. When I was awoken for my guard shift, I took my glasses out of my helmet, put them on, and they immediately fogged over and effectively rendered me blind. They warmed to my body temperature in a few moments and cleared up but it scared the shit out of me. I was temporarily combat ineffective. After that, I found I could sleep only on my back, with my glasses on, and never turn over. In the field, I never took my glasses off at night for the rest of my tour.

Between movements, when we were in a day-pause, we had a little time to relax. We could eat, write letters, read a book, play cards and talk to each other. I played chess with Doc Lewis. All of us all carried water-proof ammo cans to store our personal stuff. I kept letters from home, writing paper, a little money, paper-back books and a camera in my M60 ammo can. If we were in the flat lands, some guys played music on small cassette players they kept in the larger, 50 caliber cans. My Latino brothers like Salas introduced me to Carlos Santana and his "Black Magic Woman." Brother Tyron Pitman played Edwin Star's "War":

"War – Huh! – Good God Y'all.
What is it good for?
Absolutely nothing!
Say it again!"

I could not possibly put it better than that.

* * *

Vietnam, sitting on the west edge of the South China Sea with its monsoon season and vast rain forests, is home to a huge variety of creatures that are peculiar, perilous, and, once in a while, cute.

"Mongook" was a young mongoose. This friendly, furry little creature just walked into our daytime position in the lowlands one day as though he owned the place and instantly became the platoon mascot. "Gook" was the name used by many G.I.s for the Vietnamese people. This was a Vietnamese mongoose, so of course, he immediately became Mongook. First cousin to the ferret, the weasel, and the meerkat, the mongoose is smart and surprisingly sociable with humans. Smaller than a cat, bigger than a squirrel, this little carnivore hunted anything his powerful jaws could eat: snakes, chickens, small mammals, birds, amphibians, insects and C-rations. He really did make that "rik tik tik" sound that Rudyard Kipling described in his 1894 novel The Jungle Book. In it, he included a short story called "Rikki-Tikki-Tavi" about a mongoose that saves his adopted family by killing a pair of cobras in their house in colonial India. Because of their lightning speed, thick fur and partial immunity to the cobra's venom, mongoose vs. cobra encounters were always mongoose 1, cobra 0.

Mongook stayed with us for quite a while and was everybody's friend. When we moved, he rode on the top of someone's rucksack. Often, he would fall off - with no apparent damage - and the next guy in line would scoop him up and put him on his pack as we continued on. Unconfined, Mongook could have left us anytime he chose, but he seemed to like us so he stayed. Even though he was a wild animal, I think his presence made many of us feel better as only a pet can.

When the platoon was picked up by helicopters to move to our next AO, we lost our little buddy. As the slick climbed a few hundred feet into the air, he just stepped off the edge. I want to believe he survived the fall. There's a good chance he did given the heavy, green vegetation he fell into and his native toughness. He earned his jump wings and joined the Airborne for real, but we couldn't turn back. Our mission didn't include wild mascot rescue.

Troopers in I-Corp encountered many other exotic animals, including tigers, monkeys, elephants, deer, mammals of all descriptions, lots and lots of insects both common and exotic, and of course, the ubiquitous domesticated water buffalos.

The common scene of small children sitting atop these thousand pound beasts was an incredible sight to the eyes of a young American soldier. These very large, horned animals basically served as the Vietnamese tractor. We saw kids as young as 4 years old with a switch in their hands directing and minding the huge animals when they were not working. As shocking as this  appeared to us, this custom had been engrained in their culture for thousands of years.

The Vietnamese children in general were much more self-reliant than their American contemporaries. I remember well seeing a young girl - maybe 8 - walking along a paddy dike in charge of her little brother, who was maybe 2 or 3 years old. When the little naked toddler needed to take a shit, the girl held his hands as he extended his little butt out over the water of the rice paddy whereupon he dumped his load. A couple of quick swishes of water to clean his rear and they walked on. No disposable diapers - good fertilizer - eminently practical and efficient.

COKE KIDS

Imagine you are a grunt who's been in the field for months. You are in the lowlands near the villages on a day pause, and coming out to the platoon is a small cadre of enterprising youngsters selling - among other things - cans of Coca Cola. Better yet, on occasion they would be carrying a makeshift ice chest constructed with Styrofoam packing material bound with bamboo and holding a single block of ice. For an extra 50 cents, they will roll your coke can in a grove in the ice block and actually manage to chill it down to normal American room temperature. One dollar MPC "cool", 50 cents for ambient air temp. I don't know there they got these blocks of ice. I do know that a fairly cool Coca Cola in the middle of a Vietnam summer day is a transcendent experience for an infantryman.

We called these young entrepreneurs "Coke Kids." These children were no older than 9 or 10 and they would come out from the villages to hang around the platoon. Some were not into "sales" but just wanted to socialize with Americans. Some sold soft and hard drugs along with beer and Coke.

American soldiers love kids. I think his has always been true. It was true in WWII, it was true in Korea, and it was true in Vietnam. Adults and teenagers were not to be trusted, but the children got a special GI exemption. It's an American cultural bias. We treated these children like a different species from the rest of their communities.

I suppose it's important to note that these children were survivors. They moved within the platoon and it would be stupid to believe that they did not share what they knew with people we did not like. These children were in a position to virtually count our bullets. We would move at dusk to our nighttime ambush position to conceal our intentions but I wonder how successful we were sometimes.

The kids were, of course, fascinated by all things American. They spoke better English than their elders and taught me most of the Vietnamese language I learned. Some formed strong friendships with GIs, and occasionally an American soldier felt so strongly about one of these kids that they wanted to adopt them and take them to American. These fragile fantasies collapsed when the soldier came to the end of his tour. I've seen more than one big, strong, combat hardened trooper break into tears at the inevitable parting.

FRAG FISHING

Be a good neighbor, my father taught me. My Dad was raised in rural Florida in the 20's and 30's where my grandparents sharecropped 40 acres. In that era, good neighbors were sometimes a matter of survival. Dad surely was a good neighbor. It was a life-long habit learned the hard way during the depression. You visited the sick and you helped the needy. Every man was your brother, as another child of God, and you never did him ill, by commission or omission.

Technically, because of our location, right in their faces in the croplands, the Vietnamese civilians were our neighbors by circumstance. They lived in the lowlands. We lived in the lowlands. It wasn't a very big area.

* * *

I was sure the boy was standing on a grenade. He was doing it on purpose and there was nothing I could do. It was just another day and we received a resupply by helicopter: Fresh fatigues, C-Rations, mail, ammo, and cases of new hand grenades. We split the frags amongst the platoon to replace the old ones. Then, we threw the old ones away. More specifically, we methodically pulled the pins on the old frags and threw them into the nearest canal. Having them explode under water was safe for us and had the side effect of killing lots of fish. When we were done, the kids who had been watching us eagerly jumped into the canal to collect the fish - free food for their families. Problem was, not all of the frags had detonated.

I had been keeping track and I knew that at least two of the hand grenades had not exploded. At first, my concern was that one of the kids would disturb one and kill himself and his friends. I brought

this to the attention of the platoon leader thinking we could at least order the children out of the water but he vetoed the idea. I realized he was right. None of us was going to jump in that water and try and find those unexploded frags.

I returned to the edge of the canal and watched the kids. All of them were scrambling for the fish. Except one. This lone nine year old was standing still in the chest deep canal. That's when another thought struck me. Those dud frags were more valuable than all of the fish. I think the kid was being still and trying to look invisible because his foot was touching one of the frags. I can't prove it but I believe that both of those unexploded frags found their way to our enemy for trade or favors. We may have added a little to the local economy but I don't believe that throwing frags into the children's

swimming hole meets the good neighbor rule. There was no malice in what we did. We just didn't give a shit.

OPERATIONS

Field time for a line grunt with the 327th Infantry was divided into two major areas - the mountains and the lowlands. The mountains were by far the worst. Flat ground was rare and the jungle was dark and dense. This was double and triple-canopy jungle. The first layer was the lower growing plants that include the ground cover and range up to midsized bushes, small trees, and foliage that we had no names for. Second are the regular-sized trees of all varieties with their hanging vines. Finally, there is the upper, overarching layer of the tallest trees and nameless jungle growth towering above the lower plants. In this environment, sunlight often could not reach the forest floor.

1ST PLATOON ON PATROL NORTH OF T-HAWK. FIREBASE CAN BE SEEN ON THE MOUNTAIN TOP IN THE BACKGROUND

We were always climbing up or walking down with our heavy load, and the vegetation was oftentimes impassable. In those cases, the lead man in the platoon would have to cut a path through the bush with his machete until his arm gave out. Then the next guy would move to the front and continue cutting trail and so on. Sometimes, traveling a few hundred yards took all day. Other times, we would follow an existing trail, one made by someone who wasn't us. Green as it all was, this was no walk in the park. Every step was a risk. An ambush or a booby trap could happen at any time. You tried to see everything, tried to hear everything, and fear was in the shadows.

In the mountains it is a little cooler because of the shade from the canopy, but that is offset by the fact that there is preciously  little flat ground and you are always going up-or-down with that 100 lb. pack. When I left Vietnam, I weighed 156 pounds and could swing that pack onto my back in one clean-and-jerk motion.

When Alpha Company was not in the mountains, we spent our time in the lowlands operating right next to the Vietnamese people. The lowlands were flat and covered in rice paddies and fields. This is where most of our contact happened. We lived and operated right next to or inside the little hamlets that dotted these crop lands. Our job was to be a barrier between the villages and the enemy hiding in the mountains. We were good at it. As the farmers went about their daily lives, we patrolled through and around their villages. Every day we moved to a different location. Every night we conducted ambushes.

The firepower each man in the platoon carried was terrifying. The 327th Infantry was heavy line infantry and we were loaded for heavy battle. The stuff I carried that went bang included: my M16 rifle, 720 rounds of ammo, 5 fragmentation grenades, 2 claymore mines, 2 pounds of C4, 50 feet of detonation cord, 2 starlight flares, 2 smoke grenades, and one or two cans of M60 ammo with 100 rounds apiece for the squad machine gunner. Add in a week's worth of food, two gallons of water and all of the other stuff you need in the field and you've got the reason we were called "Grunts."

Any one of us could have personally killed every soul in a village. I was in awe of this capability. You never shake the experience of carrying so much lethal power. Our basic humanity and the rules of war kept us from using it at the wrong time - mostly.

During the daylight, in this populated coastal area of I-Corp in 1970, enemy actions were not common. We reconned for that night's ambush site and patrolled through the villages. When we weren't moving, most of us tried to take short naps. We were going to be up all night - waiting in the dark - to kill whoever walked by. If you were a Vietnamese civilian, you did not leave your home at night.

HOW DO YOU SAY HELLO?

I had been waiting for just this moment and there they were. Three Vietnamese walking in a row along the rice paddy dike. It was perfect. Our patrol was walking along the same dike in the opposite direction and I waited for my chance. I was in the middle of the squad, M-16 at the ready as always, and I waited for the man to get within about ten feet.

FLOODED RICE PADDIES

He gave me a quick glance and I seized my chance. "chào ông," I said. I tried to sound friendly and gave a small nod of my head as was the custom. I caught the shock in his face. Then he nodded back with a forced smile and said, "chào ông" ("Hello" to a man, in Vietnamese). Then it got better as my plan unfolded. The first of the three was a man, the second was a woman and the third was a young girl. The Coke Kids had briefed me on all three. As the woman - probably his wife - approached me, I said, "chào bà" (Hello to an older or married woman) with an even friendlier tone of voice and with a little deeper bow of respect. She looked scared but returned the greeting with a "chào ông" without any smile. Then the young girl - probably their daughter - approached and I gave her a big smile and said "chào cô " (Hello to a younger, unmarried woman). She actually giggled and said "chào ông" in return. All I had done was to say hello to a family using the proper gender and age. For a moment I was proud of myself - but it was a futile gesture. They had no reason to like us and my attempt to win hearts and minds was pointless. They knew why we were here. Our job was to kill anyone moving at night. The dead were often people the villagers knew or were related to; their cousins, their fathers, their brothers, their sons.

ALPHA IS FOR AMBUSH

For every ton of rice they managed to steal from the villages, we killed 6 or 7 of the enemy soldiers who tried. [xiii]

During the wet season, the lowlands were a jigsaw puzzle of flooded fields, rice paddies bounded by earthen dikes. In these pools, the Vietnamese farmers planted each rice plant by hand with the tops just above the water, until the whole paddy was filled with neat rows of young rice plants. These ponds were navigated by way of the earthen dikes that surrounded them, several feet high and hardened by centuries of foot traffic.

During the dry season, after the rice harvest, the lowlands became a patchwork of small fields surrounded by those earthen berms. Clustered here and there near the rice paddies were the small hamlets and villages - the homes of the Vietnamese farmers - arranged in no plan clear to a Westerner but somehow melding perfectly into the landscape. In this area, at night, we conducted ambushes to intercept the enemy trying to make it from the edge of the jungle, to the villages, and then back to the jungle with the precious rice.

Our company commander would spread our platoons out for maximum coverage of the many paths from the jungle to the villages. Small unit operations were the trademark of the Vietnam

War and we did almost everything at the platoon level:

15 to 25 men. I remember only two times during my tour when Alpha moved as an entire company. Platoons rarely saw one another while they were in the field. The three platoons of Alpha Company were often kilometers apart.

Our enemy, however, had one destination - the villages - and they couldn't avoid all of our ambushes all of the time. This was a true bottleneck for the bad guys. By the time of my tour in 1970, the 101st had almost cut off their access to the rice in the lowlands and they were starving. Ambushing them between the jungle and the villages was one part of our military strategy in which we were highly successful. We could have held this populated strip of I-Corp forever - and that's about how long it would have taken.

Our ambushes were setup anywhere and everywhere - along the edge of their rice paddies, in their cemeteries, along trails, beside the railroad track, within destroyed structures, and even within unoccupied houses on the perimeter of the village itself. [xiv]

After we conducted the daily recon, the platoon leader would choose that night's ambush location and, just with the fall of twilight, the platoon would move into position. Then we waited in the dark all night long, waiting to kill whoever walked by. Nobody moving at night was your friend.

You tried to peer into the darkness using your night vision. You strained to hear everything while remaining absolutely silent yourself. You could often hear the mongoose scurrying in the grass, the sound of the "fuck you" lizards with their strange, insulting call, and any creature small or large moving through the brush. More than one water buffalo became an ambush casualty. The one thing you could almost never hear was the enemy. Unlike the mongoose, they were trying to be quiet.

Sitting up at 2:00 in the morning with at least half of the platoon awake around our perimeter, you passed another pleasant night in a war zone without front lines. No two ambushes were alike. What they did have in common was surprise, intensity, and chaos. Even though ambushing was our explicit mission - and enemy action was always our expectation - there are some things you really can't get ready for.

SPARKY

A soldier in combat does and sees things he cannot get out of his head. My friend Sparky from 3rd Platoon knows this well. It was mid-July and the platoon was ambushing near Highway-1, a kilometer and a half east of the Nuoc Ngot Bridge. The platoon was lying in wait, concealed in chest-high grass, next to the trail that started at the highway and ran southeast to the edge of the Bach Ma Mountains and on into the jungle. First squad's M60 gun team was anchoring the left flank in a small clump of trees on the end of the ambush closest to the jungle. Second squad's gun team was setup on the right flank a few meters from the junction of the trail with Highway-1. Sparky and his point team were in the center of the ambush between the two-gun teams. The command post was four or five meters behind the point team. Another 5 meters behind the CP was the other point team providing rear security. All positions were in radio contact with each other.

The ambush was setup well, but as the night wore on, the watch on the left flank must have fallen asleep. A squad of VC coming from the mountains toward the highway walked right passed them without either side detecting the other.

Sparky was lying on his back on his poncho. Clifford Gibson had relieved him from his guard, and he was trying to rest while

Gibson and another platoon member stood watch and monitored the radio. Suddenly, Gibson grabbed his foot and gave it a hard shake. Sparky sat upright and immediately saw the silhouettes of men on the trail right in front of him. Flipping over to a prone firing position, Sparky aimed at the closet silhouette and pulled the trigger. Nothing happened. He had not flicked off the safety. At the same moment, the radio broke squelch and the trooper to Gibson's right began crawling quickly away from the VC through the tall grass making a terrible racket. His M-16 had jammed and he was trying to get away from the VC a few feet away. Hearing this, the enemy soldiers came to a sudden stop, dropped to a crouch, and began moving toward the noise - straight toward Gibson and Sparky.

3RD PLATOON POINT TEAM:
MARTY, SPARKY, FREDDY, JACK

Gibson fired first into the belly of the lead VC which was by then only inches from his muzzle. The man let out a loud, long groan. Sparky remembers the groan going on and on as time stood still. By now, he had flicked off his safety and he shot the second VC who was a little further away - at least two or three feet - before the VC could fire the RPG he had raised to his shoulder. Then all hell broke loose.

The gun teams at both ends of the ambush opened up with murderous M-60 machine-gun cross fire. The remaining enemy split into two groups - one running back toward the mountains and the other trying to go forward toward the highway. All of them were cut down.

In the middle of the firefight, Sparky suddenly noticed that tracers were buzzing inches over his head from behind. The RTO at the

CP was firing at the enemy with his platoon mates directly in his line of fire. Someone finally got him to quit before his "friendly" fire killed somebody.

Like most contacts, the whole firefight lasted less than a minute. Then, the M79 gunners began putting up illumination flares. Sparky and the other guys on the ambush line conducted a brief sweep to clear the area to their immediate front. Then they drew back so the CP could call-in artillery. The howitzers from Fire Base Tomahawk blasted the area along the trail back to the mountain as well as the area further to their front - just in case. A Huey soon arrived on station and took over the job of providing illumination by dropping parachute flares from the helicopter.

Rear: Seeman, FO, Thompson
Front left: Tolsty, Hodges.

After the artillery barrage ended, the grunts in the front line began a more extensive sweep. Sparky with Pat Cota on his left came upon the first body. The VC moved and let out a moan so Pat emptied the rest of his magazine - 7 to 10 rounds - into the VC on the ground. He was slamming in a fresh clip to shoot again when Sparky yelled, "Pat! I think you got him!"

They were just completing the sweep when the Huey ran out of flares. It was replaced by an airplane they called "basketball" that stayed with them for several hours kicking out flares for continuous illumination. Using this light, 4 troopers - including Sparky - were detailed to collect the enemy bodies.

Knowing the enemy's practice of booby trapping bodies, they cautiously tied a rope around an extremity of a dead enemy, backed up, and tugged the body toward them in order to trip any booby traps the enemy often left behind. After doing this to the first three bodies, the CP got antsy and they were ordered to hurry up. They took the calculated risk that the firefight was too intense and too short for the enemy to have had the time to place booby traps. So they tied ropes to whatever extremities were still attached to the bodies and dragged them back to the platoon. They tossed the 8 bodies and the various body parts into a gruesome heap. The platoon then made a perimeter around the bodies to guard them for the rest of the night.

Sparky and his slack man, Marty, were setup about 8 feet from the pile. One of the VC had his eye blown out of its socket and it was hanging down on his cheek. The eyeball seemed to be looking at them. Marty got out his field dressing, went over to the body, and wrapped the bandage around the VC's head and over the eye. When he returned, Sparky asked him what was going on and Marty told him he could not stand that eyeball staring at him any longer.

When daylight came, Sparky saw that his hands, jungle shirt and jungle pants were covered in blood. He was able to rinse most of the blood off his hands with water from his canteen but he had to wear the bloody fatigues for days until the next resupply chopper brought them clean uniforms.

It bothered Sparky that some in the platoon began taking "souvenir" pictures of the dead enemy - including taking off Marty's field dressing so they could get a picture of the eye. He thought it was in bad taste. Who, after all, would they show such pictures to back home? He also thought it was totally unnecessary. His memory didn't require souvenirs. Sparky can still hear that endless moan. He can't forget the bloody fatigues he had to wear for days. And he will see that goddamned eyeball forever.

QUICK KILL

"I felt the bullet in my chest!" Sperm's voice tightened as he spoke and I thought his eyes were looking at something only he could see. As he told me the story, it was clear the sharp edge of the memory still penetrated.

Sperm (Frank Seaman - so, aka "Sperm" - naturally) was anchoring the left leg of an L-shaped ambush as the squad machine gunner. Frank was seated behind his M-60 in position for action to his front. He was on the far-left end of the row of 2nd platoon troops making up that leg of the "L."

He's not sure why he felt the need to look behind him, but he did. Straining to peer into the darkness, he saw a shadow, a shape - and the shape was moving. It was approaching the rear of the squad, not the front the ambush was meant to cover. He began to make out the form of a man in the darkness. *Was it another member of 2nd platoon?*

As the shape came closer, he began to make out the silhouette of a boonie hat. [xv] Nobody in 2nd platoon wore a hat like that. The man advanced another step and Frank could see the curved outline of the banana clip of an AK-47. The man was only a couple of steps away.

Frank jumped up to confront the enemy with only his bare

hands. The NVA soldier was so close he had no time to swing the heavy, belt fed machine-gun weapon to his rear. The enemy soldier's assault rifle was aiming squarely at Sperm's chest. The guy had him dead bang. Frank could already feel the bullet in his chest.

Battle is a matter of millimeters and microseconds. "Look out!" he remembers saying. The trooper to Frank's right, Lt. Douglas Sherman, who does not remember hearing the warning, spun around and put two rounds through the enemy soldier's center of mass without taking aim. He immediately dispatched the slack man (the second man in a squad) with two more shots.

The platoon cherry, on his first ambush, had the third NVA in his sights but hesitated and asked his squad leader what to do. The sergeant snapped, "kill him!" which the cherry proceeded to do - thus ending his one-day career as a cherry. The fourth enemy soldier was dropped by fire from other members of the platoon.

The dry operational report the 101st HQ issued each quarter lists the ambush and body count - they always stressed the body count. It summarizes the action and notes it was by 2nd Platoon, Alpha Company, 2/327th Infantry, the time and approximate location, and nothing more. It was just another ambush report in an endless series of ambush reports. Three or four NVA kills was a routine body count for our ambushes. I know of no POWs that made it to the rear after an ambush.

Frank lived to tell me the story thanks to Lt. Sherman who saved his life with that quick kill. To this day, he still carries a small 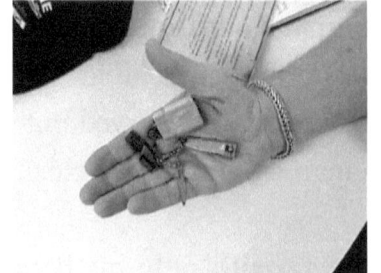 chain with the lighter, nail clippers and P-38 can opener he found in the pocket of the man who almost killed him. It is his talisman. It has power.

LIGHTNING FLASH

The platoon was moving from our day pause to that night's ambush site when a flash of lightening froze us in our tracks. No man in the platoon took another step. Twenty meters in front of the point man we saw the troops of 2nd Platoon in their ambush position - and we were walking straight into it.

We'd been hunkered down all day - under our poncho tents - doing our best to stay dry. Rain in Vietnam was not like rain at home. The drops are bigger and there are more of them. We were in the monsoon season. It didn't rain all the time. It just seemed that way.

During these days, we used our big, heavy rain ponchos to set up makeshift tents. Most of the platoon was under shelter during the day except for the occasional squad recon. We were just hanging out because our mission would not begin until dusk.

Here, in the lowlands, the jungle gave way to an open, civilized area of fields and villages. The enemy would be crazy to initiate contact during the daylight here. It wasn't because we were so damned tough, but because the enemy would receive hellfire from the nearest artillery battery within 3 minutes - less if you had experienced radiomen at both ends. Nevertheless, we kept our weapons close and our eyes and ears on. I was never more than a step away from my M16 at my most relaxed. Most of the time I held it in my hand - usually by the pistol grip. After I left Nam, every time I went outside, my right hand had an empty ache where the pistol grip should have been.

We rucked up at twilight as always but, as we began to move out, the weather went totally to shit. It had been raining heavily all day, but now it was raining holy hell. The rain wasn't falling in sheets or buckets, it was a deluge.

Somehow, we got behind the curve. Movement in these conditions was risky. Our visible horizon was clouded because of the downpour. Add in darkness and the white noise of the rain to the limits of vision and hearing and you have a recipe for disaster.

Our platoon leader was a good field commander, but these conditions made any operation hazardous. I doubt he had any choice. Division wanted ambushes - period. As far as I could tell, Command didn't ask what we thought about it.

The Lt. took point and we threaded our way along the network of rice paddy dikes. It's a bit like walking around the edges of the squares on a checkerboard except these squares were not aligned. The pathways on top of the dikes were compacted by many years of use by the Vietnamese farmers. They were wide enough for foot traffic or a water buffalo but little else. In the dark and the rain they seemed a lot narrower.

You could see your hand in front of your face, but not at arm's length. How the LT could make out the path is a mystery to me. Maybe he couldn't. We were feeling our way and moving slowly which also made us late. The platoon should have already been set-up in our night position.

After moving what seemed way too long, we made a left turn onto the next square and were approaching the next intersection. The front of the platoon was a few feet short of the intersection when the brightest, coldest and luckiest lightning flash of my life illuminated the surroundings. For an instant, God's flashbulb let us see twenty-five yards further and revealed the tops of the poncho shelters of our own 2nd platoon. Without the lightning flash, we would have walked straight up their position.

The men ahead of me all saw the same thing at the same time and we stopped cold in our tracks. After a moment, the Lt. turned platoon around and we moved back along the route we had come from and away from the ambush. Clearly, more walking around was not a good idea.

We retraced our steps a couple of hundred yards back where the path left the top of the dikes and ran straight along the side of the paddies for fifty yards. There, we made our night defensive position on the trail. There was cover to our rear and clear fields of fire at nine, twelve and three o'clock. Not perfect but good enough.

We wrapped up in our ponchos and poncho liners and slept on the muddy trail. The heavy rain continued through the night, but the very light though very warm poncho liners inside the rugged ponchos kept us fairly comfortable.

Friendly fire incidents on night ambushes were well-known amongst the grunt's word-of-mouth network. Usually these happened between squads within the same platoon who got disoriented in the dark. They rarely occurred between different platoons as nearly happened to us this night. These incidents did not make it into the reports - but the grunts knew.

DAISY CHAIN

My buddy Ricky Mendez from 2nd Platoon was part of the biggest ambush I know of. Rick was a 19 year-old draftee from New York by way of Puerto Rico and had seen his share of combat. He was part of a six man sniper team operating in the mountains about 4 kilometers south-east of FSB Tomahawk. On the fourth day of their ten-day sniper mission, they had ring-side when T-Hawk as attacked. Rick and his team could see T-Hawk in the distance during daylight, and at night they could see the occasional flicker of light from a cigarette. Rick said that the battle was quite a fireworks show.

The team was immediately withdrawn back to T-Hawk the next morning and given a new mission. They were briefed on a new ambush technique and given the mission to intercept NVA troops expected to withdraw through the area they had just been in. Maybe the intelligence came from one of the POWs we captured on Tomahawk, or maybe it was just a logical choice based on the geography.

There is no doubt that the NVA being targeted were from the same battalion that hit the whole Phu Loc AO the night before and had awakened me so rudely. Ricky and the team moved back into the bush within hours of the briefing with a new specialist added to the team. He was not a grunt, but knew how to work the remote, wireless detonators they were going to try for the first time.

The mission was to deploy a line of claymore mines along a little buffalo trail where the enemy was expected to pass. The squad quickly setup 24 claymore mines, spaced 20 feet apart, and connected to each other by detonation cord in two groups of 12 claymores. This created a huge kill zone 160 yards long.

The final connection of the wireless detonators was done solely by the specialist who was probably a guy from S-2 (intelligence). Then, the squad withdrew to a safe observation post (OP) half a klic or so back from the trail, where they had a clear view of any movement. They wanted to blow the daisy chains when the maximum number of the enemy were in the kill zone.

The six men in the team took turns watching the trail. On the first day, they didn't see anything. Then, the second day after T-Hawk, they struck pay-dirt. Rick had just finished his shift from the OP. He turned the observation duty over to Dougy and laid down to try to catch some shut-eye. After a minute, Dougy suddenly said sharply. in a low voice, "Mendez! Do trees walk?" Rick looked up just as the NVA point team was coming into view. Sure enough, they looked like trees walking. Our enemy was very good at camouflage, but since "trees don't walk," as Rick said, he knew it was time for the shit to hit the fan.

He got on the radio to alert the guy with the detonator and told him they were going to let the point team pass and try to get the main element. After the lead team passed, Rick counted at least thirty more behind them spread out in combat spacing. Twenty were within the kill zone and more were entering. Rick was waiting until a few more entered the zone before giving the final command to fire. He said over the horn "I want you to fire . . ." and paused but the word "now!" never left his lips. The guy pushed the button immediately and the first daisy chain of 12 claymores blew as one. Ten of the NVA were killed immediately, and that many more were wounded. Artillery from T-Hawk began pasting the trail to catch the fleeing NVA who were beginning to run past the second set of claymores. Unfortunately, shrapnel from one of those blasts cut the connection to the second daisy chain before they could detonate it and they missed the chance to kill the second lot. Altogether though, it was the most successful ambush I heard about, and had the added benefit of payback.

OH MY GOD

Long before we saw her, we heard her wailing. "Ou Chúa Wi," "Ou Chúa Wi," Ou Chúa Wi." Later, I would learn from the coke kids that those Vietnamese words meant, "Oh My God, Oh My God, Oh My God!"

My platoon was patrolling along Highway-1 when we heard the woman's lamentations. Soon, a group of 2nd Platoon guys came into view. In front of them were the bodies of two young men who had walked into that night's ambush. On her knees before the bodies was a middle-aged woman. She knew these young men. Was she their aunt, their sister, their mother?

She was rocking back and forth as she wailed. On the forward rock, she patted both her hands on the bodies and on the backward rock she raised her arms and screamed to the heavens. This scene - dumping the night's kills on the highway for disposition by the Vietnamese - was a daily occurrence in the No Slack AO.

The distance from the ambush sites to the highway was not far. Sometimes the platoons would carry their kills in ponchos with a trooper at each corner. Sometimes they would tie the hands and feet together and hang the body from a pole. Sometimes the kills were simply drug by the feet over open ground with a rope or a length of claymore wire. If there were too many to be moved to the highway by the platoon, they would send a Chinook helicopter and take them out in a cargo net. Since the bodies started out in various states ranging from simple bullet holes to serious mutilation, by the time the bodies were dumped beside the highway the condition of the corpses was sometimes a bit degraded. The intestines might have spilt and trailed behind in a grisly rope. The head might have fallen off. Arms and legs might be missing.

I thought of the woman grieving over the young men dead by the side of the road when I first heard General William Westmorland's famous quote. [xvi] "The Oriental doesn't put the same high price on life as does a Westerner. Life is plentiful. Life is cheap in the Orient." I think he was trying to give excuses for the miserable failure of his "search and destroy" strategy.

He was right about the difference in the value placed on life between us and our enemy. We spent vast sums of money and 60,000 men. They spent comparatively little money but much more of their most precious resource - their people. This is what was required to prevail. And so they did, at a cost of millions of their lives.

GATHERING VEGTABLES

We loaded her body into a poncho and lifted it onto the chopper. Her legs we put into a second poncho and tossed those aboard too. She was dead by the time the slick arrived. It had taken about 20 minutes. Doc did his best but both of her legs had been sheared off cleanly right at the pelvis. I don't think there was even any way to put a tourniquet on her. I do not know if her children were injured. At least they were all on foot, running back to the village, ages around four, six and eight I would guess. I think their mother must have been just far enough ahead of them to save their lives.

We had been in the mountains for a week and had just gotten back to the flatlands. The night defensive perimeter we setup was just inside the edge of the jungle. Another 20 meters and you would emerge into the land of people and rice paddies. We were bone tired, dirty, and some of the other guys stunk to high hell. After a week in the steep, deep bush, returning to the lowlands was always a relief. Tonight we would sleep a little easier. There was no ambushing to be done this night.

At dusk, just before last light, the platoon would set claymore booby traps on the likely approaches. My squad drew the duty. Claymore mines were an anti-personnel staple of a grunt and the weapon of preference for perimeter defense. We all carried at least one and they were used in two different ways. The standard mode was a deliberate, command detonation. The blast sent a wall of steel ball bearings in a fan-shaped arc propelled by three quarters of a pound of C-4. That is devastating to anything on the business side of a claymore. You can also use them to cut down small trees.

The booby trap version we called "mechanicals." We used a field expedient trigger consisting of a clothes pin or two halves of a plastic C-ration spoon rubber banded together to make a spring loaded firing device. Each arm of the trigger was wrapped with copper wire attached to a battery and a plastic spoon handle was inserted between them to keep them apart. This last spoon was attached to the trip wire. A tiny tug on the trip wire would pull out the separating spoon and close the circuit that was powered by a battery. Boom!

The night was uneventful. Shortly after sunrise, one of our booby traps blew. The sound of a C4 explosion is not like an explosion as most folks think of it. It's more like a huge giant slamming an enormous hammer on the ground. We moved out in combat formation - cautiously. We assumed enemy activity.

I have had claymore booby traps go off because a bird landed on the trip wire or because the dew got the triggering device wet or for no goddamn reason at all. This time it blew because a young woman - I'm going to guess about 25 years old - walked into it and had both of her legs blown off.

When we got to her I could see her children running back to the village. I never saw their faces - just the back of their heads in order of age - the 8 year old in the lead followed by the 6 year old followed by the 4 year old.

Lying on her back before us, their mother never said a word - never made a sound. I wouldn't find out until she was dead that she was pretty. Now, her face was twisted in silent agony. I knew she was conscious because her eyes were clenched shut so fiercely. All of the muscles of her face were as tight as a human being's can be - especially her mouth. There was no sound, no whimpering, no crying, and her body moved only a little with pain she could not contain. So it was as the life slowly left her and finally softened her face.

After a few minutes, the whole damn village came marching out toward our position. The Vill was about 300 yards from our NDP. Coming down from the mountains and stopping within the edge of the jungle for concealment, I don't think we knew the village was there until the young mother walked into the booby trap.

An old man with the long beard - the village elder - led a crowd of 40 or 50 villagers, probably the entire population of this little hamlet. All of these people - hurrying to find the source of the children's panic - were her neighbors, her family. I'm sure they were desperate to help the mother. We would not let them approach.

We put up a quick open field perimeter - lying prone, rifles to the front - and sent the Kit Carson interpreter out to talk to them. I can't remember if we fired over their heads to keep them back but I know for sure they were not going to breach our perimeter.

The woman had been carrying a small cloth sack, a little paring knife life such as you would use to peal an apple, and some twine. She and her kids were clearly out there to gather some kind of wild plant or such for their pantry.

I could see the platoon leader and the squad leaders in a huddle staring at this stuff. I imagined they were hoping those little things she carried would somehow turn into a satchel charge or something that would identify her as an enemy.

The chopper showed up and as quick as we could we put her aboard and they lifted off for the 95th EVAC hospital in Dan Nang, which was only 10 or 15 minutes away by helicopter. With that, the villagers withdrew and we moved out.

I was in a surreal universe where the normal rules of civilization did not apply. I saw, I noted. I did not feel. My heart was filled with lead. The grief - the guilt - would come later.

DINNER WITH THE FAMILY

I don't think I would have actually shot those two GIs, but I think they thought I would. I wasn't thinking it through anyway. One way or another, they were going to stop messing with that fourteen year-old girl. There are only two other grunts besides me that know this story and I'm pretty sure they won't tell. There is also a Vietnamese family who will remember it well.

The picture you see here is of a modest little Vietnamese house that our platoon occupied for an hour or two. At this point in the war, an intact, middle class home like this one was increasingly rare. You can see our packs both inside the house and on the front porch. You can also see the little Vietnamese homemaker tending some bush and trying to pretend we weren't there.

Why did we occupy these houses? I have no idea. Maybe just to get out of the sun. I was just following the leader and there was no obvious tactical reason, because we just hung out and left after a little while.

On a day that blurs with the rest, I was walking drag so I was the last one to enter a home just like the one pictured here. The rest of the platoon had gone to a back room and there were only two GIs still in the front room when I came in.

Between them they had pinned a beautiful young Vietnamese girl I would put at about fourteen years old. They were pawing her and indulging in pleasant conversation like "Hey Baby San. Wanna Boom Boom?!" (Vietnam GI slang for intercourse) while they put their hands on her. I honest to God do not remember their faces but I know they were cherries.

What seized my attention was is the naked fear on the girl's face. I could also see her father's face across the room - frozen in anguish. He was helpless. What was he going to do? There was a fully loaded platoon of the 101st Airborne in his house.

I stepped further into the room and was going to walk passed them. As I did so, I told the two guys to "leave her alone" in a rather tired, flat tone of voice. They looked at me, laughed, and continued their explorations of the young girl's body.

Maybe I had been there too long, maybe my attitude had gone to hell, but this kind of shit was not going to happen in front of me. I stopped dead in my tracks, spun to face them, leveled my M-16 at the chest of the nearest guy, and repeated the command in a low growl, "Leave! Her! Alone!" I wasn't kidding for a heartbeat and they could see their death in my eyes. They stopped cold, turned, and left the room with a couple of backward, under-their-breath mutterings to save face. There was no hint of a challenge.

An older woman - the mother or the aunt or whoever – came in and snatched the girl away from the room in the blink of an eye. She got her the hell out of that house and down the road to a place of safety somewhere else in the village. I finally dropped my ruck in a corner and sat down to take five alone in the front room.

What happened next is one of my few cherished memories of that goddamned war. I wasn't paying attention to anything at that point except being tired when the father of the house came back into the room and walked over to me. He was smiling and saying something pleasant or grateful or something. Then, the damndest thing happened. He reached down where I was seated, took my hand, bowed and motioned to the next room – the dining room. He was inviting me to have dinner with his family.

I grabbed my ruck and weapon and stepped into the room where there was a long, low table that seemed rather full of food. The father guided me to the center of the table. I leaned my ruck up against the wall behind me, propped my 16 on it, turned my back on my weapon, and sat down on the floor. There were four or five other adult family members already seated, smiling quietly, waiting to begin the meal.

I felt as a guest that I should bring something to the meal, so I turned around and dug into my ruck. I fished around and came up with a can of C-ration "beans and franks" and I opened it with my P-38 can opener. I figured they probably thought I was going to eat it in lieu of their food but I set it on the table far enough from me that it was clear that it was intended to be my contribution to the meal. I didn't have a bottle of wine after all.

Then the conversation began in earnest. The Vietnamese like to talk - at least to each other. They passed me rice and fish and I think something that was chicken. We ate and smiled and said shit to each other that neither could understand. "Your country is very beautiful!" I said with a big smile. The family responded to my words with lots of nodding and smiling and spoke pleasant sounding words in return that were as gibberish to me as mine were to them. We kept up this friendly dialogue while I made yummy sounds about the food. More smiling and nodding and talking and smiling.

It was all over in maybe 15 minutes. For fifteen minutes, I was not an invader in another human being's home. For fifteen minutes in the whole fucking war, I was a guest in the home of a grateful father.

NOBODY SEEMS TO KNOW

I knew something was wrong with the kid even before I could hear him. My platoon was in our daytime defensive position, resting up for that night's ambush. His platoon was passing in front of us, walking along a rice paddy dike with standard five meter combat spacing. The slender, blond-headed trooper was in the middle of the twenty man platoon from Bravo Company that was moving to our north.

Anything out of place - in this place - drew your immediate attention, and this soldier was clearly out of place. The young man was not alert - not ready for combat action. He seemed to be completely unaware of his surroundings. It was like he was in some kind of a trance.

His gaze was fixed on the ground. He held his rifle loosely at the end of slack arms, one hand around the fore grip, and the other around the narrow end of the stock. When an infantryman is moving in the field, he always holds his M-16 by the pistol grip so he only has to make a small movement of the thumb to click off the safety and begin firing.

His head moved slowly from side to side as he walked along the earthen berm. First down and to the left, then a brief pause, then to the right, another pause - then back to the left. When his platoon got a little closer to us, I could hear him talking to himself.

"Nobody seems to know!" He said to no one. Then that pause and a slow turn of his head to the other side.

"Nobody seems to care!" Then, the next pause and he turned his head back.

Over and over with each turn of his head, never lifting his eyes from the ground, he repeated the words. "Nobody seems to know. Nobody seems to care." As he did this, he changed the inflection - perhaps in an effort to get it right somehow. Sometimes his voice was flat. Sometimes it was emphatic. Other times it sounded like a question, then like pleading. Mostly it was resigned. All of it sounded lost.

His platoon moved on and out of sight but the kid stuck in my mind. My first thought was that they needed to get him out of the field. He sure as hell wasn't doing any good, and his mental absence put him and others in danger. Then it struck me that in his disillusion and bafflement, he was speaking not *to* us but *for* us. *We* understood. *We* cared. It was everybody *else* he was talking about. He said out loud what all of us were feeling. In our guts, we believed that the majority of the American people did not have a clue what was going on here in Vietnam, and frankly, most of them did not give a shit. How else could we reconcile their apparent apathy in the face of our horror? Most of the citizens of the United States went about their business and only got involved in the war by watching a five minute segment about the Vietnam War on the nightly news. Otherwise, they conducted their daily, civilized lives with no skin off their ass unless they had a son or a husband or a brother in Vietnam.

Their taxes did not go up. They were in no danger. They didn't have to spend any time working for or against the war unless they were motivated by an unusual social conscience. The struggle, the waste and the futility they were putting us through didn't seem to reach their awareness. In a sense, they were in more of a trance than that young soldier. We were in a separate dimension - a different universe. They were in the "World" while we were in "The Nam." Grunts had to adopt a grim indifference to make it.

"It don't mean nuthin!" we said to each other. *"It don't mean a goddamned thing!"* was the reply we gave.

FISHING WITH KIT CARSON

I'd gotten used to Kai. Kai was our Kit Carson Scout. He had been with us a long time and I liked him. I also respected him. It bothered me that Kai took a lot of school-kid abuse from some of the guys in the platoon - you know, the shoving, horseplay and domination games guys play in high school, but he always laughed and never, ever lost that smile. And we stayed safe while Kai was with us. I  think I know why he was smiling. He was at least ten years older than the guys in the platoon and I understand he had been an officer with the NVA.

Kit Carson scouts were with all the platoons of our battalion. They were former enemies who took advantage of a special program called "Chu Hoi" or "Open Arms." Leaflets with the offer were scattered from helicopters all over the jungle. The deal was simple. Switch sides, renounce your affiliation with your former comrades, go through a bit of training and reorientation, learn the value of democracy and allegiance to the wise leaders of South Vietnam, and then you get to go to the field with an American platoon and tell them where to go or at least how to get there.

The idea that these Kit Carson scouts - who had been our enemies - would now help lead us to victory could have come right out of Joseph Heller's Catch-22. The notion was stark, raving mad. However, it didn't take me long to understand the upside.

I finally figured out that, as insane an idea as thinking that these "converted" VC and NVA soldiers would help us find the enemy was, the underlying brilliant idea was that this same Kit Carson scout could probably do a pretty good job of avoiding contact with his former comrades. The one thing that the enemy wanted to do the least was engage an American infantry platoon. We were tough targets and they almost always came out on the short end. They would much rather fuck up the ARVNs and leave us alone unless they had no choice or a very specific strategic mission. That was an idea that suited me quite well.

By this time in the war, we were well on our way out and everybody knew it. The troop levels had been drawn down by more than 25% just since I got here and for the grunts "search and destroy" did not make nearly as much sense as "search and avoid." The US had decided to shit-can this place and was just trying to pretend we hadn't.

For the first time since I joined the platoon, we had a second Kit Carson scout with us. His name was Troung. I don't think Troung liked us. You could see it in his eyes. We had them both for a time - I assumed it was so Kai could show Troung the ropes. We sure as hell couldn't speak Vietnamese, and I'm pretty sure they had some other things to talk about.

Troung worried me though. I wasn't sure he got the memo about the avoid thing. He was much bigger than Kai, nobody fucked with him, and he most definitely did not smile. His face was flat and expressionless but his eyes were hard.

One day in the mountains, we were in deep jungle and had come to the end of the day's march. We dropped our rucks and were beginning to setup for the night when I saw Troung walking off down the trail by himself. He was walking in the direction we had been headed in and hadn't seen yet, and I wondered what the hell he was doing. I followed him, staying 20 yards behind, to see what he was up to.

After a few minutes and a couple of hundred meters, the trail passed next to a stream. Troung stopped, stripped off his pants and waded into the thigh deep stream. I stopped maybe 10 yards back, sat down on a rock, and watched.

He knew I was there but he never acknowledge my presence. What he did do was to reach into the water ever so slowly, ever so carefully and then froze with his arm in up to his shoulder. After a few moments, he made a sudden move and stood up with a fish in his hand. He smacked it on the head, tossed it onto the bank and returned to his fishing pose.

In the space of about 5 or 10 minutes, he caught 3 more fish and 2 turtles. He then waded out of the stream, put his pants back on, gathered up his catch and walked on past me back to our night pause. He never looked at me.

I followed Troung back to our night defensive position, and there Kai had been doing his part of the chores. He had strung up their two hammocks while Troung caught dinner. They had fresh fish and turtle and we ate our c-rations. They slept in their hammocks off the jungle floor and we slept on the ground with bug juice to keep the leaches off.

These two "defectors" were as close as I got to knowing any or our enemies personally, and that knowledge was not reassuring. We were humping 100 pound rucks with a week of food canned for the military, transported to us halfway around the world, and finally kicked out of a helicopter to us below, all at incredible cost. Troung got enough food for two guys, for two days, buck naked in the middle on a jungle stream. This was our enemy.

BLOWING UP THE TRAIN

They could have blown up the train with fewer explosives but I think they were showing off. There was so much TNT under the track that the old, iron locomotive was blown straight up into the air. I smiled even though it wasn't funny, certainly not to the train crew. Rather, it was a grim smile, a smile of grudging respect. I felt the sublime futility of what we were doing and the simple elegance of what they were doing. And they did it right in front of us.

Los Banos Perimeter

Guerilla warfare - what the smart guys today are calling asymmetric warfare - is a bitch. The thesis is simple and profound. It's asymmetric - unbalanced - because the two sides have vastly different firepower.

The military of the United States of American in 1970 was hands down the most formidable fighting force that had ever existed in the history of the planet. After 25 years of the cold war, there was literally no place on earth we could not go,

and almost none we could not dominate against any conventional force. For that matter, there was no place in Vietnam we could not take and hold against anything the enemy could do. We dominated the air. We had the supplies, logistics and manpower to establish artillery bases anywhere we needed to. And we had lots of tall (or at least taller than them), healthy, well-fed, well-armed combat troops to kick Charlie's ass pretty much anytime they tried to stand up against us or we just happened to stumble on to them. It is no small matter that overall in the war we killed 10 of the enemy for every one of our dead. That's an important fact and an honor to the American soldiers that did it. It is also an honor to those enemy we killed, for unlike us, they did not die in vain. They achieved their goals. They won their war.

The theory of guerilla war is to hit and run. You defeat your enemy with the death of a thousand cuts. You wear him down. You travel light and you live off the land. You pick the time and place to hit your enemy when you can do the greatest damage with the least risk. And you keep this up for as long as it takes, for decades if necessary. It is not a strategy for the faint of heart. Only guys who are deeply committed, tough, and really pissed can pull it off. Our Vietnamese enemy was all three.

* * *

It was an ordinary day in the fall of 1970 and 1st Platoon was assigned to perimeter security at Fire Support Base Los Banos. "Los Banos" means "the baths" in Spanish. I thought that was a good name for that particular fire base since it was one of the few places in Vietnam where we got to take a shower. The shower was little plywood box exposed on the southwest edge of the hill with a cold-water tank on top but, there was soap, and the water was actually clean. When you haven't had a decent bath in several weeks, even this primitive setup was welcome.

Relaxing on a firebase was about as good as it got for a grunt in the field. A two or three-day stay on a firebase was pretty close to heaven compared to the other twenty-seven days of the month. Out of the jungle. No humping. No ambushes. No booby-traps. Hot food sometimes. And a place to sleep that was out of the goddamned rain. I loved fire bases.

Fire bases were comparatively safe except at night. The enemy didn't attack fire bases in the daytime - at least not very often. That was suicide for no purpose and that's not the way the enemy fought the war. When they did attack a fire base it was for a very specific reason.

On this particular fall afternoon, we were feeling quite content, kicking back and taking it easy. We would be on 50% alert all night but during daylight the mood was pretty relaxed. I was lounging in a fighting position attached to a perimeter bunker on the gulf side of the hill, taking in the view, and sharing a bowl of dew with one of my buddies when the train came into view to our east. From our hilltop vantage point you could see the train several miles away, puffing its puffy steam smoke. It approached from the base of the Hai Van Pass, skirted the edge of Lang Co Bay, and then passed through a tunnel at the base of our hill. The west end of the tunnel was no more than 500 meters away from where we were sitting. After it passed through the tunnel, you could watch for another couple of miles as it chugged its way to the west and finally disappeared.

Chugged is the right word. The picture of the train here is not a mistake. It really was an old fashioned, 19th century steam engine. It would have been perfectly in place in a John Wayne western set in the 1870s. This was a South Vietnamese train - you couldn't have gotten a GI to board one at gunpoint. It carried the stuff of Vietnamese commerce - rice, fish, pigs - and ARVN troops and military supplies.

There were diesel trains in use in Vietnam, but there were also lots of these turn-of-the-century throwbacks. It was more of the Nam's otherworldliness - not only out of place but out of time as well. In Vietnam we had the Stone Age (literally hunter-gatherer), subsistence agricultural (water buffaloes included), the industrial revolution (steam engines optional) and the highest tech weapons in the world, all mixed into a mind-bending soup. We called the United States "The World" for a good reason. The shit here in "The Nam" was not for real.

To understand the importance of the train and the larger truth it demonstrated about the respective strategies of us versus our enemy, you have to consider the terrain in this part of Vietnam. Our Division Area of Operations (AO) extended from north of Da Nang to the DMZ - basically all of Thua Thien and Quang Tri provinces. My battalion had responsibility for the portion of the AO from FSB Los Banos to FSB Tomahawk near Phu Loc. Along this very narrow strip of land runs the single highway and the single railroad track next to it. It was a true bottleneck. We called this stretch the "bowling alley." It was our job to protect it.

The 101st Airborne Division had two missions in Thua Thien province. First, secure the population centers in the lowlands. Second, find and destroy the enemy hiding in the jungle. The first mission we succeeded in and probably could have kept up forever. The second could never have been accomplished. Not with the six hundred-thousand men we had, not with a million men, not with 3 million. For the most part, the enemy fought us where, when and how they wanted to.

Sitting on top of Los Banos, my buddy and I watched the train make its way along the coast toward us. When it got to our hill, it disappeared into the east end of the tunnel at the base of Los Banos, and after a minute or so, came out the west end of the tunnel that was directly downhill from our position. At that very moment, I turned to my buddy and said, "You know, it's been about a month. That train is due to blow." He nodded and we turned back to watch the train. It continued on for perhaps another 10 seconds before it rose silently, gracefully into the air. The sound of the explosion followed a moment later. It was beautiful. It was awful.

The train, like all of them, was pushing several flatcars ahead of the engine to trip charges before the main body of the train got there. So this explosion had to be hand-detonated. We watched the little bitty figures of the VC who had done the deed - at 500 yards away they looked like little ants - running as fast as their little legs would carry them along the rice paddy dike that led from the railroad track to the edge of the jungle. They covered that 200 yards in about half a minute and were gone. They were never within M-16 rifle-range. There was no time to bring anything else to bear. This train was destroyed for free.

* * *

I spent 14 ½ months in Vietnam and during that time the enemy blew up a train on that track about once a month. My forecasting the destruction of this particular train on this particular day was no more fortune telling than it is when you guess the phone call is from a friend you are sort of expecting to hear from anyway. This small cadre of VC - maybe six guys - only had one job: to blow up that train. I have no idea how much time, effort, tax dollars and human resources the 101st put into trying to stop the enemy from blowing up the train but it was wasted.

The fact of the matter was that we were never going to be able to secure that rail corridor. The enemy could pick any place along 25 miles of track. They could bide their time, hit from the jungle and run back to it; they could have kept it up forever. Our efforts were expensive and futile, theirs were cheap and effective, and nothing we did could stop them.

GARBAGE RUN

I watched the little children - some barely more than toddlers - fight and scratch and bite one another to get at our garbage. Dante couldn't have made this hell up. This was something we had created. From where I was standing, no one from MACV down seemed to give a damn about the stain on our honor. This neglect was not benign.

* * *

We'd been ambushing in the lowlands for several weeks. As always, most of us never knew what was coming next. The platoon leader got directions from the company commander. The Lt. passed the necessary information to the platoon sergeant, and he in turn to the squad leaders. What generally ended up at the end of the chain where the rest of us were was "ruck-up and go this way." Sometimes we were told how far - "two kilometers north" - so we could say, "oh shit." As always, it was out of the blue when we were told we would be getting a break on a fire base. Back to FSB Los Banos again where there was cover from the rain, a little mess hall, and it was mostly quiet.

Fire Support Base Los Banos anchored the south end of our

AO and Tomahawk anchored the north. The one road between these two firebases ran almost exactly east to west - a rare straight stretch of road - for 10 kilometers. In between these two ends of the "Bowling Alley," there were only scattered hamlets, rice paddies, graveyards and not much else. Beyond these, the road was flanked on the East by the South China Sea and on the West by the jungle-covered mountains.

The sole permanent position between T-Hawk and Los Banos was the Nuoc Nogt bridge – pronounced, "Nook Knock." The Nuoc Ngot ("sweet water") river had this one crossing point to accommodate train, motor vehicle and foot traffic. Both South Vietnamese soldiers and Americans had duties at the bridge. The Americans occupied positions to defend the bridge but it was the South Vietnamese who controlled the crossing point.

* * *

My squad leader called me over on the second day and told me I was riding security for a garbage run. This means a 2 ½ ton truck (a "duce-and-a-half") would be loaded with garbage and other refuse and driven to the nearest dump. That was a hill near Phu Loc just few of miles north of the Nuoc Nogt bridge.

For anyone who doesn't know, Americans are the most wasteful people in the world. We throw away countless useful things. We throw away enough food to feed another large country. The US-Army as an institution is the worst.

We four grunts took positions at the corners of the truck bed, which was ringed by wood slats. It was half full of miscellaneous trash and garbage. The truck driver and a cook rode in the cab. I was expecting a nice ride and a soft detail.

We drove down the narrow dirt road from the top of the hill to the intersection with the paved Highway 1. There, we would turn toward the garbage dump near Phu Loc - about 10 kilometers to our west.

At the intersection, we saw a group of four young Vietnamese. It seemed to me they had been waiting there for us. Three of the kids - two girls and a boy - were pre-teens. The fourth was a girl about 16. She said her name was Love.

* * *

Love was possibly the most strikingly beautiful young lady I had ever seen. She was also by definition an outcast in her own world. Mixed race children were shunned in Vietnam as they are in other places.

She was half Vietnamese and half French. At about 16, it was easy to do the math. It was the summer of 1970. The French colonization of Vietnam ended in 1954 when they were defeated by Ho Chi Minh's forces at the valley of Dien Bien Phu. This girl had to be one of the very last offspring of France's occupation of "French Indochina" as it was named on the maps.

The Portuguese were the first Europeans to establish a permanent settlement in Vietnam, in Danang in 1535, but it was a French Catholic Priest (Pigneau de Behaine) who convinced King Louis XVI in 1787 to take Vietnam by force. By 1861 the French were granted exclusive rights by Emporer Tu Duc to three provinces in Vietnam including Saigon, given complete control of Vietnam's foreign policy, and Catholic missionary work was legalized.

When the French were crushed at the battle of Dien Bien Phu, the rest of the world - and especially the United States - rushed in to say "hold it just a minute." The Vietnamese and the Great Powers gathered in Geneva and forged an agreement for the future of

Vietnam. There would be a ceasefire, a temporary separation of the warring factions at the 17th parallel (The "DMZ" - Demilitarized Zone), and most vitally, national elections would be held in July of 1956 'when Vietnam would be unified into a single entity.

Those elections never took place. President Eisenhower was advised by the CIA that Ho Chi Minh would surely win by a huge margin. Ho was a commie and we all knew that they would take over the world if we didn't stop them. So the US and the Vietnamese in the south - the local colonial power structure setup by the French - decided that the elections agreed to in the Geneva treaty and signed by all parties would not be held. The right of a people to self-determination was thrown overboard in the face of cold war politics.

America had been paying for half of France's war and now we took on the full cost in the hope we could save the South from communism. The French themselves warned us not to do it but, well, they were French. We just knew we Americans could do better. We were just 9 years from our victory in WWII, the colonels from that war were the generals now, and they knew the American military was invincible.

* * *

The guys in the truck cab were permanent personnel on Los Banos and they seemed to know Love. She asked the driver for a ride to Phu Loc, he said OK, and I began to feel vaguely uneasy. We drove uneventfully along the Bowling Alley. I actually enjoyed the sight-seeing. There was no jungle near the road and an ambush was unlikely in this area. This lightly populated stretch framed by the ocean and the deep-green mountains was quite beautiful. You could almost forget there was a war on here.

Then we reached the ARVN checkpoint at the Nuoc Nogt bridge. The checkpoint was a typical ARVN military outpost: a few small buildings, lots of sandbags, a bunch of wire, a guard arm blocking the road, and a platoon or more of ARVN infantry.

These South-Vietnamese soldiers were held in disdain by many GIs. Their battle history was pathetic and their motivation was absent. After our combat troops left Vietnam, the NVA rolled over the ARVNs in a matter of weeks as if they were men of straw.

The driver stopped in front of the guard arm and expected to be waved right through. Then, the Vietnamese officer in charge - a lieutenant - saw Love sitting between the driver and the cook. Suddenly, in loud and angry Vietnamese, he ordered the girl out of the truck. The driver said no.

Then the Vietnamese office got really mad. His orders gradually reached up the scale to something approaching a scream. The ARVNs on both side of the road began to finger their weapons and my routine detail changed to "Oh Fuck!"

The ARVN lieutenant continued his furious rant. His men shifted nervously into position with their M16s at the ready. We didn't know their intentions toward this young woman but we did know about their loathing for half-breeds. Given her age and beauty, I feared the worse. We were all enlisted men - nobody with rank was amongst us - so we were in complete charge of this detail.

They were wimpy, surrender monkey ARVNs. We were the 101st Airborne and she was in our custody. They could only remove her from the truck by killing us. I made an ostentatious show of turning my upraised M16 to one side so they could see my thumb slowly, deliberately clicking my fire selector switch to rock-and-roll (full automatic). Then I lowered my weapon not at but near the ARVNS on my side of the truck. My platoon mates did the same.

This was not a Mexican standoff. It was not close to an even matchup. We were 6 GIs and they were only a few dozen ARVNs. Our respective attitudes were universes apart. We were fully prepared to blow them all away if they tried to take the girl by force. They had no stomach for a fight and they could read the determination in our eyes. After a few more moments of posturing by the officer, he cooled down, they opened the guard arm and we drove on.

After a couple of miles, we reached the dirt road turnoff to the dump just before the village of Phu Loc. Love got out and continued her journey, a short walk to the village, and we continued on to the dump a few hundred yards to the northeast.

Awaiting us at the dump was a gaggle of many young children - none over the age of 10. Young Vietnamese - particularly boys - did not approach GIs after puberty. They knew we would consider them enemies.

As we approached the dump site on top of former firebase Hill 88, the children began to swarm toward the truck. We were slowing to a few miles per hour but the children were already pressing against the sides of the deuce-and-a-half and trying to hop aboard.

I was afraid they would be crushed under the double-wide wheels so I fired a 5 round burst - well over their heads - to try to keep them back until we stopped. The children froze in their tracks for maybe two seconds and then resumed their rush. They knew I wasn't going to shoot them. Americans didn't deliberately kill children. The rare exceptions prove the rule.

We had almost slowed to a stop when the kids poured aboard. We didn't have to toss much of anything off the truck. The kids were tearing through the garbage at warp speed, fighting, pushing each other aside, and competing for the best stuff - particularly the food.

It was all over in less than 5 minutes. Very little trash and no food actually ended up in the dump. The Vietnamese could build a house out of C-Ration cartons, scraps of wood and corrugated tin.

You'd think we could do better with community relations but our mission was about killing the enemy - not helping the people. The relative budget spent on weapons versus help for the Vietnamese was 95% to 5%. Our leaders said our mission was about "hearts and minds."

Bullshit.

COMMAND AND CAUTION

I don't know when or how it happened, but silent words must had passed through all levels of command. The unspoken words said to keep the American casualties down while we withdrew. Most platoon leaders and company commanders now saw their primary duty as protecting their troops until this whole bloody mess was over.

Vietnam had become a completely different war than the one we started in 1964. It was now a defensive war, fought by men who knew it was lost. We had lost the support of the American public, the American press and the United States Congress and we all knew it. Each and every soldier in Vietnam - career soldiers, shake and bake officers, and draftees - just wanted to survive. They knew their sacrifice meant nothing. "Search and destroy" had been abandoned in favor of "search and avoid." Fortunately, the enemy was playing the same game and for the same reason. American force levels had been going down for over a year. Both we and the enemy were just waiting for the last GI to leave.

Captain Gerry Seidl

Rather than sending whole units home at one time, the Army maintained the pace of withdrawal by not replacing those soldiers who did go home. The ranks just got thinner. By August of 1970, Alpha Company was under strength by 30% or more. An Army rife platoon should have 30 to 40 men. My platoon would reach a low of 15 men with no officers. An infantry company, at a minimum, should have a Commanding Officer (CO), usually a Captain, an Executive Officer (XO), usually a 1st Lieutenant, and a commanding officer for each of the 3 platoons, usually 2nd Lieutenants, for a total a five officers.

In early August, we had one field commander - the Company Commander, Capt. Gerry Seidl. Shortly after he took command of Alpha Co., my Platoon finally got a replacement platoon leader, Lt. Steve Dahlgren. Both Seidl and Dahlgren were what I called "real" soldiers - Airborne Rangers committed to the army and its objectives as a lifelong mission.

Lt. Steve Dahlgren

The rest of the company was run by NCOs. These sergeants, given the responsibilities of a platoon leader, were more experienced than any new shake-and-bake 2nd Lieutenant freash from the states. I felt more confident when Sgt. Berry or Sgt. Beasley was leading the platoon as opposed to some new officer who couldn't read a map. Then, there was Joe Hooper who had just been assigned to my company. Joe was a staff sergeant who definitely could read a map - and he was looking for trouble. He was given command of 2nd Platoon.

JOE

I met Joe on Fire Base Los Banos after I got back from the garbage run. He was sitting on a pile of sandbags on the top of the firebase. A group of Alpha Co. troopers were standing in a loose semicircle and he was holding forth about his exploits. My initial impression of Joe was that he was a braggart. I can't recall all of the exploits he thrilled us with - the countless body counts, the boldness, the bravery - but I recall almost exactly what he said just before I walked away.

He said, "So, you just send me to the A Shau with a 45 automatic (which he carried and was fond of spinning) and I'll come out in a week and there'll be lots of dead gooks in the A Shau." Quote, Unquote. It was a nutty, offensive thing to say. Most of the men in front of him had been to the A Shau Valley and he hadn't. These men weren't smiling. They just stared at him with, you know, that stare. This was his first day with my company in the field. All I could think was "Oh Shit! What are we going to do with this guy?" One guy joked that we should put him out front and we - from cover of course - would just say, "There's one over there Joe!" and "There's another one Joe!" The guy was pantomiming a scurrying action depicting Joe dispatching one enemy after another while we pointed them out. This is, in fact, what Joe wished. To become the most decorated soldier in the history of the USArmy. Arguably, he achieved his goal.

I soon discovered that Staff Sergeant Joe Ronnie Hooper was a recipient of the Congressional Medal of Honor - our nation's highest military decoration - for his actions during the Battle of Hue in February 1968. [xvii] He was 101st Airborne - a squad leader with Delta Co., 2/501st Infantry - the "Delta Raiders." His MOH citation [xviii] reads like an Audey Murphy war movie. It describes Joe as single handedly charging and destroying multiple machine gun positions, engaging in hand to hand combat, rescuing fallen comrades and receiving multiple wounds which he disregarded to save his men. Joe was sent home and President Richard M. Nixon personally hung the sacred medal around Joe's neck in a solemn ceremony at the White House.

While back in the US, Joe was given duties that included speaking before civic groups, recruiting young men, and general public-relations stuff that the military uses to solicit support. He hated it. [xix]

The Army command did not want Joe to return to Vietnam but Joe had different ideas. This hero stuff was the biggest thing that ever happened in his life and he wanted more. He insisted on returning for a second tour - and he was assigned to my company. It had been more than two years since his MOH decoration in February of 1968 and the situation had changed. Joe had not gotten the "avoid" memo.

Joe was boastful and self-aggrandizing, which by itself is merely a personality disorder. However, saying openly that his quest for another medal was a higher priority to him than the lives of his platoon mates is inexcusable. Joe exhibited a foolish disregard for danger that imperiled his fellow troopers. Bragging and boasting is something I didn't think MOH recipients did. I do not question Joe's valor. The battle of Hue in 1968 was one of the most intense actions of the Vietnam War and there were witnesses to his actions.

A troubling story about Joe's time with Alpha Co. came from my friend Steve ("Bear") Miles. Bear was still the Alpha Co. supply sergeant when Joe arrived in the "No Slack" rear. Both he and Joe liked cars, drinking, and fighting. They hit it off immediately. Joe and Bear "liberated" somebody's jeep and drove the 50 miles south to their destination - the bar at the China Beach Rest and Relaxation (R&R) Center in Da Nang. When they entered the bar, which was as good a military bar as there was in Vietnam, a mix of guys from Army, Navy and Marines were there enjoying their drinks.

Whether it was planned or spontaneous, when Joe was sufficiently lubricated, he stood up and loudly announced to the bar's patrons, "A Marine ain't a pimple on an Airborne's ass!" He obviously started a drunken bar fight for the fun of it.

The MPs eventually broke up what must have been a historic brawl. Bear was a formidable figure even when he was sober, and I don't know if it's fair to call Joe fearless, but he certainly had a complete disregard for danger. They were tossed into the Da Nang hoosegow and released the next morning to the No Slack Executive Officer - a major who was not pleased to have to drive to Da Nang to take custody of the delinquents.

Back in the No Slack rear, the XO lectured them about dignity, decorum and discipline as they sat in an empty mess hall, nursing their hangovers and bruises, pretending to pay attention. Joe and Bear knew that nothing was going to happen to them. Bear was on his third tour and Joe was an MOH recipient. Generals had to salute him. The fact that Joe was a staff sergeant this late in his careers speaks to his opinion of military discipline. Joe had been in the army for 10 years and had made rank and been busted back many times - usually for being absent without leave (AWOL) in the pursuit of women and good times.

Joe's rear echelon behavior was irrelevant. His behavior in the field with Alpha Company was not. Because there were no officers, he was in complete charge of 20 of my fellow troopers. And, Joe was hunting.

Riding on a truck from Eagle to Tomahawk in early August, Rick Mendez had no idea who the E-6 sitting beside him was. He didn't know Joe's name or that he was a Medal of Honor recipient and he certainly didn't know Joe was about to become his field commander. Rick said that Joe was very quiet during the ride to T-hawk and the subsequent chopper lift to join second platoon - until he stepped off the bird. Then, he became Joe - boisterous and bossy. Joe wasn't interested in anything the other members of the platoon had to say. He said, "this is not the way to do things." Then he began making up his own operations. Joe started going out for his very own daily recons. He took Rick and one other guy on forays into the bush with only their rifles and two spare magazines and he would lead them as much as 4 klics away from the platoon into the mountains covered with triple canopy. The mission of Alpha Company at this time was ambushing in the lowlands between the jungle and villages to keep the populated croplands secure. We were a blocking force - not a long-range patrol - not a search and destroy operation and definitely not with 3 lightly armed soldiers led by a man looking for trouble. Joe was running his very own search and destroy missions. "Half the time he had no shirt on - wrapped around his waist - he was not communicating - just telling do this do that - no opinions." As Rick said, "This was his own shit. It didn't come from the old man [company commander]."

Sergeant "Rebel" John Simmons was a squad leader in 2nd platoon who had been in-country longer than Joe and had covered much more terrain. The Rebel nickname was well earned since John still called the Civil War the "war of northern aggression." When Joe took over the 2nd platoon, Rebel John was the senior NCO - also a Staff Sergeant equal in rank to Joe - with experience, savvy and commitment to his men. I later discovered that Reb had two passions. As the grandson of eastern European immigrants who had escaped the postwar tyranny of the Soviet Union, Reb was a fierce enemy of communism and had volunteered for Vietnam to aid in their defeat. His second passion was his love for his men and the US Army. He was tough as nails and took bullshit from nobody.

He and Rick had been together in second platoon for some time and they had seen their share of action. Rick told me about one an operation near the A Shau where they had setup their NDP. When it was totally dark, they got an urgent radio message. The message, to put it simply, was "don't even breath." 700 NVA regulars were passing within 40 yards of their position. They didn't breathe - and survived the night.

Their mission on one particular day was to be a blocking force in the edge of the deep bush. Enemy activity was always anticipated along the trails and they made good ambush locations. This was the kind of jungle where you moved very slowly, threading your way carefully through the trees and the wait-a-minute bushes, and sometimes the only way to make headway was to cut a trail with machetes. The other way to move was to follow a trail - a trail you did not make - a trail where you were expected. Ambushes on a trail - generally triggered by the point man - were one of the signature tactics of the enemy - and both Joe and the members of the 2nd platoon knew it.

You gain a feel - a situational awareness - of the jungle when you have been in it long enough. Rebel John knew it was not advisable to follow the trail. Joe knew it too so he ordered the platoon to do just that. Reb and Joe had a little disagreement. After what I'm sure were kind and diplomatic words, exchanged with civility and temperance, Joe said the words Rebel Jim will never forget. "Every man in second platoon is expendable for a cluster on my MOH." Joe was saying - in so many words - that he wanted to be the first man in history to get a second Medal of Honor. He not only did not give a shit for the lives of 2nd platoon, he was so fuck nuts that he thought he could be that lucky. He also was crazy enough to say it - in the field - to a platoon of armed men to whom he had just said the most unforgivable thing one soldier can say to another. Rebel John said nothing. He just ignored the order

Joe took off down the trail. Nobody was sure who was in command. Four of the 2nd platoon troopers followed Joe including Rick, Jack, Lou, and a 4th trooper. Rick later described that "what he [Joe] was doing was freaking the fuck out. He was actually being conspicuous. He was gonna draw some kind of contact. He was fucking like on vacation. No sneaking around. Out in the open. Maybe the enemy just didn't want to fuck with us. They could have gotten us so easy. How many times do you think they had us in their sights?"

The rest of the platoon followed the Reb as he began cutting trail with his machete to get off of this trail and setup a proper ambush. Then, Reb ran smack into a hornets' nest - literally a nest of hornets - the insect - an event of cosmic improbability. He was stung multiple times by the angry hornets. He went into anaphylactic shock almost immediately. Rebel John's throat was swelling shut, his face ballooned with the allergic reaction and his breathing became difficult. He was going to die. This was a situation that required an immediate dust-off.

Joe, who had by now returned to the platoon, was pissed off at Rebel John. According to some of the platoon, Joe initially refused to call the chopper. The soldiers of 2nd platoon advised Joe, with words and action that will forever remain secret that he was indeed going to call the rescue helicopter. The dust off came in time and Rebel John survived.

Joe was not with Alpha Company for long. He popped in and popped out, as Rick said, and he only had to do about 10 days with Joe in the field over a period of a month. One of the last straws for Joe happened back on Firebase Los Banos. Lt. Dahlgren and one of the squad leaders were disposing of old hand grenades on the backside of the hill and Joe joined them. The way you dispose of a frag in the field is, of course, to set it off. The three of them were methodically pulling the pins on the frags and tossing them a safe distance down the hill where they exploded - thoroughly disposed of.

Then, Joe pulled the pin on a frag, held it in his hand for a couple of seconds, and threw it up into the air, resulting in an airburst that, through the grace of God, only slightly wounded the squad leader - a small piece of shrapnel in his abdomen.

Steve Dahlgren and our company commander, Captain Seidl, were both real soldiers, and do not fully reveal what happened among the company and battalion leadership, but Joe was suddenly gone from Alpha Company. He was transferred back to his old unit, the 501st Infantry, where he was promoted to lieutenant.

THE HAI VAN PASS

Draftees like me were forced to be here. Once here, however. a draftee grunt fought and suffered the same as any soldier. When you're in the bush, political opinions don't mean shit. I believed the war was unwinnable from the beginning. There was no disillusionment in my heart - only bitterness and rage.

I think it must have been very difficult for the real soldiers - career military men dedicated to honorable service - men who believed in the military and its mission. And here they were - handed this piece-of-shit war and troops that did not want to fight it.

In the beginning, it was inconceivable that American military power - 20 years after our victory in World War II - could be stopped by anyone on earth much less a backward, peasant army from Southeast Asia. We didn't factor in the enemy's grim determination and their willingness to suffer enormous casualties, over several decades, to achieve their end of driving foreigners from their soil. (Insert X Factor from Why Vietnam Matters). We had to learn the hard way. For the first 5 years of the war, in major battles like Ia Drang, Dak To, Ke San, Hue, Hamburger Hill, Firebase Ripcord and others, they bore casualties of 10 or 20 to one and the bastards just would not admit they were licked. After Ripcord, in July of 1970, we stopped trying.

Gerry Seidl was the only company commander I got to know even slightly. He initially struck me as an upper-class frat guy. Turns out that's exactly who he was - his fraternity was at UCLA. Only a year older than me, he was - unlike me - committed to military service - an Airborne Ranger. He had an ebullient personality and was liked by the men. His job - Alpha Company's Job - was "to continue to provide territorial security for the accomplishment of pacification and development in the populated lowlands; deny the enemy access to the populace and resources in the coastal areas; and to seek out and destroy enemy forces, base areas, and cache sites."

This is what we did until the end of Capt. Seidl's tour with Alpha - we secured the lowlands and made occasional CAs into the mountains to look around for stuff. After Capt. Seidl left No Slack in November of 1970, the 2/327th moved north to the Firebase Birmingham AO and conducted patrols until I left Vietnam in March of 1971.

I remember during one of our company size movements along QL-1, the sudden crack of a rifle round over our heads caused the whole company to instantly go flat. Was it a sniper? Was it an errant round fired by some ARVN - famous for their weapons skills? We didn't know. After a few long moments, Capt. Seidl stood up first. Then, he made a long, sweeping forward motion with his arm and said - in his best John Wayne impersonation - "Kaka Wasa, Kawa!" in a fake American Indian dialect. It was funnier than hell and we all understood the command to go forward.

When his tour ended in November of 1970, I had the honor of driving Gerry Seidl to Da Nang to catch his ride home from Nam. We drove the 50 miles from Camp Eagle to Da Nang with just the two of us in a jeep. If it hadn't been for the war, I might have noticed that this was one of the most scenic stretches of road in the world.

As we traveled south, the lush, jungle covered mountains were on our right - strikingly beautiful if you weren't thinking about who was in there. On our left was the vast expanse of the South China Sea. From Phu Bai to Lang Co, the land is mostly flat. You pass the villages and farms and people that gave Vietnam its ancient agrarian character. Without a war, it was quite beautiful - even serene.

Then, you come to the dreaded Hai Van pass. This single road connecting I-Corp to the rest of Vietnam is a tactical nightmare. The road up the steep mountain pass is bordered on both sides by jungle that comes within a few yards of the road. We were two guys alone in an open jeep and there were no other forces with us. An ambush from the dense jungle could have been pulled off by a couple of ten-year olds with rocks. These thoughts kept me from marveling at the incredible vistas of the Gulf of Tonkin as we rose upward from the flatlands behind us.

Despite my trepidation, we reached Da Nang without incident. Then, three things happened I will never forget. First, I got to eat a hamburger! Second, Capt. Seidl bought me a drink of scotch which was equally welcome (although I did feel a bit out of place in the offices club wearing one of Capt. Seidl's shirts). Most importantly, I had a chance to have a long conversation with Gerry Seidl - the only such candid talk I ever had with an officer. We spoke, as equals, about the war and, although he didn't ask, I could tell he wondered how the troops felt about his time in command. So I told him, "you kept the men safe - and they all know it." He didn't say anything in return but I think I saw a smile of satisfaction. He had fulfilled his mission.

I GOTTA GET OUT OF THIS PLACE

OLD MAN

I knew I'd been there too long when I started hunting. It had been more than a year since I arrived in Vietnam and everyone I knew had gone home. The new guys scared the shit out of me. Too many Cherries. Too many dirty weapons. Too many loose attitudes. I didn't trust them.

It was January of 1971 and the troop reductions had been going on since June of 1969 - a year and a half. Nobody was coming to Vietnam who thought we were going to win this war and nobody wanted to die for nothing. Morale suffered.

It had only been five months since the siege of Firebase Ripcord, the last major battle of the Vietnam War. We could still run into trouble. Ripcord was less than 10 kilometers west of our current position. In November, Alpha Company's AO moved to the general vicinity of Fire Support Base Birmingham which sat astride the invasion route from the Au Shau Valley to the biggest prize of all, the ancient imperial capital, the City of Hue.

After Ripcord, the US military really stopped trying to win the war. Instead, we line grunts were performing patrols in the areas around major installations and basically securing our withdrawal. Our leaders - military and civilian - just wanted out with as few additional casualties as possible. That didn't mean you wouldn't walk up on the enemy or that they left us entirely alone. They never stopped testing, but they were patient. They seemed to be content with the pace of our withdrawal. It gave them time to build up men and material for the conquest of the South once we were gone. Ultimately, they let us go. "Peace with Honor" was what President Nixon called it.

I started walking point every time we moved. I wasn't ordered. I just picked up my stuff and went to the front of the platoon. I was the platoon's old man. No one objected. They didn't know what the fuck they were looking for anyway. I just hoped their rifles would fire.

There was something else. For the first time, *I wanted* to find the enemy. I don't know how to explain it except to say that I felt I had *insufficient war*. Others had *so* much more. I was ashamed of being in less danger than them. And I only had three months left.

THE SACRED WATERING HOLE

By the time we setup Firebase "Volkswagen" in February of 1971, the platoon was down to 15 men. We had three 4 man squads and the CP - the platoon leader, his RTO and the platoon sergeant. The United States had withdrawn more than 100,000 troops from Vietnam in the year since I arrived, but the area of operations for the 101st remained the same. We were just spread thinner and thinner.

It wasn't really much of a firebase and it wasn't really called Volkswagen. We named it that because it was so small (also because VW were the initials of the platoon leader but that is another story). We were joined by one three-man mortar squad for this mission - 18 guys on a little hilltop. We were only able to setup a 4 position perimeter with 3 men in each foxhole to cover the CP and mortar squad in the center. It was a one night minifirebase with one mortar tube. As always, I had no idea why we were there.

It turned out to be a very long night. The first mechanical booby trap blew about 2300. The second one exploded a few minutes later. We were being probed. For the next couple of hours, we tossed grenades at staggered intervals from each foxhole, every 5 or 10 minutes, to dissuade whoever was approaching. We never saw the enemy and the next morning we found no trace of whatever tripped our booby traps.

* * *

We moved off the hill after dawn. About midmorning we paused and I joined 3 other guys on a water run. The map showed a stream a few hundred yards to our south, so the 4 of us gathered all of the canteens we could carry and made our way to the stream. We crossed road 547 and saw a long, low stone wall that surrounded a large area of many acres. We walked through a gate in the low wall, and right into a holy place.

It was still the jungle but it was different. The large trees were all there, but the wait-a-minute bushes and the slash-you elephant grass were not. This place was tended. It was more like a park. It was probably the prettiest spot I saw in Vietnam.

After another 200 yards, we reached the edge of a large pond. It was so beautiful I almost expected a white swan to swim into view. The rest of the squad got busy filling the canteens at a clear spot that seemed designed for this purpose.

My attention was riveted on the school. It couldn't have been anything else. The structure was about 30 meters square. It was made entirely of wood and stood two stories tall. On the East and West side there were solid walls while on the North and South side there was no wall whatever and the building stood open to the jungle. On the South wall a staircase led to the upper story.

The upper floor and the roof above it were supported by dark, polished, wood pillars - possibly teak - possibly mahogany. Ten feet tall, they were fluted at the tops and bottoms and they were shaped as on a lathe - narrower at the base and top and widening at the center. The roof resting on the second set of these columns was intricately carved and up tilted at the eaves in the Vietnamese custom.

The floor was a lighter wood burnished to a dull luster. Even though it was open to the jungle, there was no dust nor leaf nor blade of grass on the floor. There was no furniture, no wall decorations, and, other than the 4 of us, no human being in site.

I knew we were being watched. The monks had seen us coming and quietly melted away, but not too far.

I knew this was a school because of the purposefully built layout. The two large rectangular areas - one on the bottom floor and one on the top - were the schoolrooms. I could imagine the senior monk seated in front of the East wall facing West and the younger monks in rows to his front facing him as the ancient knowledge was passed in this most real place in Vietnam, unchanged for over a thousand years. There was certainly a monastery nearby and probably a temple as well, but they were not visible from here.

I climbed partway up the stairs to the second floor - far enough so I could see the upper floor with just the top of my head cresting the stairway opening. Then I felt an overpowering sense of violation. My dirty jungle boots were making tracks on their perfect stair steps. I backed out in shame.

I circled the whole building once and returned to the squad who had just finished filling their water bottles. I don't know if they'd given any attention to the school. They were getting ready to move out and I had to hurry to get my canteens filled. The squad was already on the move when I finished my last canteen.

Then, I saw the most puzzling thing. As I screwed the cap on the last bottle, I shifted my focus to the bottom of the shallow watering spot. There - on the bottom - was one perfect human turd. Not a cylindrical meat eater turd but a vegetarian turd that sat there like a perfectly round shit pie. Why was it there? Who did it? This had to be deliberate. Was it meant as a deterrent? Did it mean "don't get your water here you dumb-ass GIs?" I'll never know.

As I stood up to leave, I caught a flash of saffron among the jungle green. I turned and saw the torso of a youngish monk - about my age - standing just at the edge of the clearing, half concealed by the bush. I stared at him for a moment and he stared right back. Then, I bowed toward him in what I took to be the Buddhist way as if to say "sorry about disturbing your holy place." Then I hurried to catch up with the squad, which was almost out of sight.

I did not mention the turd to anyone else. We always put plenty of water purification tablets in all water we got in the field. Given all of the disgusting things in those slow-moving, warm waters of Vietnam that we drank, vegetarian monk shit was probably one of the better ones.

B-HAM

My R&R to Bangkok, Thailand happened just in time in February of 1971. My ten days in that most appropriately named city was a surreal respite. I came back to Vietnam with no desire to return to the jungle and just a bit of attitude slippage.

Making my way from Thailand to Saigon to the Hue/Phu Bai Airport, I arrived at Fire Support Base Birmingham. It was located alongside the Perfume River that ran east to Hue and flowed into the South China Sea. It was called the Perfume River because of the vast stretches of fruit trees that lined its banks and filled the air with their sweet fragrance. When we patrolled its banks, there was no perfume.

Mobley and 1st Platoon on Fire Base Birmingham. Perfume River in the background

The trees were still there. Dead pole after dead pole after dead pole as far as you could see. Devoid of leaves, they stood in mute testament to the effectiveness of the Agent Orange herbicide. The US military killed off practically every green thing along the entire invasion route of the '68 Tet. This was our AO and the herbicide - dioxin - was in the soil we slept on, in the water we drank, in the air we breathed, and I'm pretty sure it was a spice in our food.

The green that had returned was primarily chest high Elephant Grass that sliced any exposed skin with its tough, saw-toothed edges. You wore your sleeves rolled down, in spite of the heat, or you suffered the consequences of the thousand cuts.

I came to B-Ham to catch the weekly supply chopper, which was the only way I could get back to my platoon in the field. As a transient, I was not directly under anyone's command on B-Ham. Not being kept track of for a while means two things. Don't bring attention to yourself, and keep it up as long as possible. Once they know where you are, they will ask you to do something.

There was a dug-in row of bunkers near the perimeter on the east side of the fire base - as far away from anything else on the base as you could get and still be inside the wire. These were used to billet people coming and going to Birmingham and were meant to be occupied for only a day or two by troops in transit. Several of the bunkers, however, had been turned into a kind of semipermanent halfway house for problem soldiers some commanders in the rear didn't want to deal with. These guys were, of course, natural allies and I fit right in.

I missed the first resupply bird I could have taken back out to the bush. That gave me another week to kick back. I'm pretty sure I wasn't the first soldier in history who took the long way home.

OLD FRIENDS

On B-Ham, I ran into my former platoon leader, Steve Dahlgren, and another friend, Allan Kentalla. I was strolling past the area behind the Birmingham Command Bunker when a jeep came tearing up the road to the top of the hill. The jeep was driven by Allan whom I knew from my days in the rear. Allen worked for S-2 when I worked for S-4. In the rear, among the intelligence officers, Allan presented as the perfect soldier. Boots shined, fatigues starched, cap neatly in place, he looked the pride of No Slack. We became friends because he was a guy I could talk to and he liked the guitar. I hadn't seen him for seven months and he had been transformed.

FSB Birmingham Command Post

I have no idea how he came to be with my former platoon leader but Allan had gone totally bush. He wore a Boonie hat, necklaces with beads and peace signs were around his neck and there was definitely no starch in his fatigues. He looked like any grunt in the field - just like me. That may also have had something to do with what was in the little utility trailer behind the jeep he was driving.

Three pith helmets - the mark of regular NVA soldiers - were lying in the trailer. They were a tad blood spotted and all had nice, perfectly round holes the size of steel ball bearings that had recently gone through their wearer's brains.

Lt. Dahlgren practically leaped out of the jeep and was hurrying toward the command post. I barely had a chance to say "Hi", catch his trademark grin, his return greeting, and he was gone. Steve was hands down the best platoon leader of the five I had in Vietnam and I sort of wanted to catch up with him, but he had duties - I'm sure to report the enemy activity to the senior officers in the CP. He told me later that he was in a hurry to get to his R&R but I think it had something to do with the fresh kills and a wee bit of adrenaline.

Allan filled me in about the ambush that yielded the pith helmet trophies. It was a claymore ambush - a favorite or Nam GIs - which confirmed the source of the nice round holes - and the kills were in our close vicinity. The NVA regular army forces were running patrols almost within rifle shot of where Alan and I were standing at that moment - two more months before I could go home. Super.

TARGET PRACTICE

1st Platoon was still a day or two away from B-Ham when I decided to check the sighting of my M16 (called zeroing your weapon). The row of bunkers that housed us transients was right behind the line of fighting bunkers that guarded the perimeter of the fire base. Beyond those fortified fighting positions was no-mans-land - the space between the bunkers and the wire. This bare, bludgeoned ground - perhaps twenty-five yards wide - had seen many actions. I was walking slowly and carefully in the area looking for small things - little sticks of wood or pieces of war flotsam - to use as targets. Then I saw it. Half buried in the dirt and barely visible was the round top of an unexploded hand grenade. The thought formed in my mind almost immediately. *Can you detonate a hand grenade by hitting it with a round from an M-16?*

I found a stick a few inches long and carefully placed it directly behind - but not quite touching - the frag. I stood up to continue my search and saw another half-buried frag right away. The truth is that, on average, in any batch of hand grenades, there are a surprisingly high number of duds. Maybe as high as five or ten percent of all those thrown do not go off - probably because of a flaw or damage in the fuse system. All of the explosive, however, is still there. I found and marked a half dozen more dud frags, backed-up to cover just outside of the blast radius of an M-4 fragmentation grenade, and put my steel pot on. It took two or three shots before I hit the first frag. The result was a most satisfying *"Boom!"* I was grinning when I aimed at the second frag. One shot this time. Boom! The next took two shots. Boom! The fourth I think was one or two and the fifth I can't remember for sure but it was no more than three. You kinda needed to hit them dead-on.

My experiment was proceeding nicely when I heard the shouting behind me. "What the fuck are you DOING!?" A portly Master Sergeant was huffing down the road that led up to the CP at the crest of FSB Birmingham. When he got close enough to hear me, I said, "just zeroing my weapon Serge." "Well fucking STOP IT!" he shouted. He just stared at me for a moment and turned around to walk back up the hill to the commander who had dispatched him to investigate the ruckus. It was only then that it occurred to me that I had been - unintentionally - creating a pretty good sound simulation of light contact. You know "bang, bang, boom, bang," etc.

I've wondered how many others have used hand grenades as targets - on purpose. Probably not many, but I can't believe I'm the only one. It's such an obvious idea. Anyway, I confirmed the zero on my M-16.

MEDIVAC

I was Medevac'd from Vietnam. Not because I needed to be, but because the Army insisted. It did not occur to me for a split second to argue.

Alpha Company was back at Eagle for a three-day stand-down. We got to shower, eat in the mess hall, sleep under a roof, and even see a movie. There was a nasty rumor circulating that we were headed back to the A Shau Valley. This was not welcome news at any time and worse when you only have three weeks left in-country.

I joined a pick-up baseball game in the No Slack rear. They needed a catcher and I took the position even though I wasn't really qualified (I was a water-polo player). For a couple of innings, I thought I was doing pretty well. Then, the very qualified pitcher burned in a most excellent fastball - which I caught - but which also nicked the tip of the index finger on my right hand. The pain was instantaneous and I excused myself from the game. The finger began to ache and I could not move it.

My platoon leader listened skeptically to my story but sent me to battalion aide anyway. Those guys took an x-ray and pronounced my finger just fine. I thought that was great but I still couldn't move it. Battalion aide sent me to Division aide.

The techs there took two more x-rays from different angles. Now, you could clearly see the bone wedge that had sheared off from the face of the last joint and was suspended between the two sides of the joint. I had broken my trigger finger. I swear it was an accident.

After the techs pasted the film on the light board, the doctor came over. It seemed to me he had been there way too long. His face was emotionless and his bearing was resigned. I don't think he ever looked me directly in the face.

He glanced at the x-ray and sat down on the bench in front of me holding a clip board. Staring at it, he asked me "what's your MOS?" I replied, "eleven bullet." "How long do you have left in-county?" "Three weeks." Without looking up, he scribbled something on a paper and said "OK, you're going home." Then he stood up and walked away without another word.

I instantly went out of my Vietnam mind. After the medics fitted me with a padded, aluminum finger split, I floated back to my battalion, never touching the ground, and straight into the S-1 (administration) shack. The clerks had already been notified by division and they were cutting my orders before I got there. Bless their pea-picking hearts! They had them ready in an hour. Still removed from place and time, hovering in my bubble, I drifted on to the Alpha Company area to grab my duffle bag. I saw no faces. I spoke to no one. I said good-bye to no one. By now, we didn't know each other's names anyway.

Orders now in hand, I marched directly to the Hue/Phu Bai airport - just on the other side of the road from Camp Eagle. Even though I showed up as a sudden standby, I got a seat on the very next C-130 to leave I-Corp for Saigon. No more than four hours had elapsed since that fastball.

I was on a military medical transport out of Ton Su Nut Airport the next day headed for Okinawa. Only after I was on the plane did

I finally read the orders the S-1 guys gave me. Among them was the award of a Bronze Star. To this day, I don't know why.

The Army only does things one way - the Army way. Since a doctor sent me home, I had to go through the regular medevac channels. This meant flying in a cargo plane refitted with litters along the sides and canvas seats for the walking wounded. The plane was full. A trooper next to me was missing all of the fingers on his right hand. The guy on my other side was adjusting his colostomy bag where his intestines used to be. Most of the guys in the litters didn't move at all. And, there I was, with my finger splint firmly in place - perhaps the only guy on the plane who did not earn a Purple Heart. I felt like dog shit. The funny thing is; every guy I talked to smiled at my story and seemed amused but delighted by my good luck. They - the really wounded - let me off the hook. I will never be more humbled than I was then.

The trip back to the World went from Saigon to a short stay at the Army Hospital on Okinawa. Since I required no treatment of any sort, I just wandered around the hospital grounds. I can't say I saw much of Japan.

Most grunts going home were issued a new Class A uniform with blue cord on the right shoulder that only the Infantry could wear, the appropriate awards and campaign ribbons, and shiny new boots. I left Vietnam wearing the same jungle fatigues and jungle boots I came out of the field with. Since I wore hospital garb in Okinawa, I got the fatigues laundered at the hospital laundry and wore the fatigues on to America.

It was dark when we landed at Travis Air Force Base northeast of San Francisco. Fourteen months and seven days had passed I left from the same base. I checked in to the base hospital and, since I still needed no care of any kind and had no duty responsibilities, I was free to leave the hospital until Taps.

I checked out at the nurse's station and, as I turned to leave, I caught sight of a television screen on the wall of the lobby. It was the first TV screen I'd seen in a year and a half and I was momentarily stunned. It wasn't *real*. I was instantly offended, and I wondered why. For two years, I had lived in each moment. There was no pretense, no role playing, and the realities of each instant were inescapable. I stared at the television screen, and through it to the American culture it symbolized, and I was appalled.

In some ways, it was a cultural shock as profound as the one I experienced stepping out of the door of the plane on my arrival in Vietnam. The bridge to Vietnam was sudden. I was seized and cast halfway around the world in a comparative instant. Now, the bridge back to the World stretched before me. The bubble that had formed around me had changed into a black box and I couldn't get out of. I didn't know this country or my place in it. I did not how to cross this bridge. I never really could.

I marched to the closest place on base that had a bar. I don't remember if it was an officer's club or an NCO club. Even though I was only a Spec-4, I seriously didn't give a shit. Still in my jungle fatigues, with Vietnam mud on my boots, I strode to the middle of the bar, sat down, and ordered a double scotch on-the-rocks and a beer. The bartender took one look at me and served the drinks.

THE END

EPILOGUE

I was against the Vietnam War from the very beginning - before ground troops were committed. The war was a mistake of historic proportions, prosecuted by the nation I love. There are critical lessons to be learned from America's misadventure in Vietnam. Our best-in-the-world system of government acted out of ignorance, arrogance, hubris and narrow political and economic interests. The people of this nation were flatly lied to, and that is not a matter of opinion. The consequence of those lies was a continuation of the war far beyond what the American people would have otherwise tolerated. The strategic and tactical consensus of our best military leaders was hopelessly flawed, and their stubborn pursuit of a failed strategy in the face of the truth on the ground is inexcusable.

The rage that burns in me is about betrayal.

It's about the betrayal of our soldiers and their honor by the people for whom they fought and died.

It's about the United States government's betrayal of the American people by lying to them about the purpose and progress of the war.

It's about America's betrayal of the Vietnamese people, promising them liberty and then abandoning them.

It is rage at myself for betraying my values by participating in a war I believed was harming my country, something I swore I wouldn't do.

It is most of all about the betrayal of our sacred democratic principles. Those principals transcend our interests as a nation. They belong to all mankind, and they proclaim the right of a people to determine their own destiny.

* * *

On May 27th, 1964, the President of the United States, Lyndon Baines Johnson, was worried about the quandary of Vietnam he had inherited from his predecessor, John Kennedy, and he called his National Security Advisor, Mc George Bundy, to unburden himself. This is what he said:

> "I'll tell you," said Johnson, "the more that I stayed awake last night thinking of this thing . . . I don't know what in the hell - it looks to me like we're getting into another Korea. It just worries the hell out of me. I don't see what we can ever hope to get out of there with, once we're committed. I believe that the Chinese Communists are coming into it. I don't think that we can fight them ten thousand miles away from home . . . I don't think it's worth fighting for [my emphasis] and I don't think that we can get out. It's just the biggest damn mess that I ever saw." [xx]

Those were not the words of a President considering the survival of his nation - or even its vital interests.

Two months after he said this, President Johnson would inflate a fabricated incident in the Gulf of Tonkin into a national emergency, and at his request, on August 7, 1964, the Congress passed

Public Law 88-408, the "Southeast Asia Resolution," better known as the "Gulf of Tonkin Resolution." The 1964 election was less than ninety days away.

The Vietnam War as we call it or the American War, as the Vietnamese call it, could not be won for two reasons. First, the nature of the enemy we faced. They were fighting on their home ground, with crystal-clear motives, using innovative strategies, and with the commitment of their people to rid their country of foreign domination. We were fighting far from home, in unforgiving terrain, using outmoded strategies, without clear motives, and worst of all, without the commitment of our people or a vital national interest.

Second, the place in which we faced them. It really was a jungle out there; a dense, dark, dangerous, primeval goddamned jungle. The jungle was an instrument of our defeat as surely as our enemy was. Whoever thought we could win a war there, in that place, against those people, was either ignorant or deluded.

General Vo Nguyen Giap's four-step strategy depended upon the jungle. They didn't even try to keep it a secret. Giap said it quite simply, "If the enemy advances, we retreat. If he halts, we harass. If he avoids battle, we attack. If he retreats, we follow." All they had to do was to keep it up. And that's exactly what they did, for over thirty years.

Ho Chi Minh told the French in 1946 "You will kill ten of our men, and we will kill one of yours, and in the end it will be you who tire of it." [xxi] This is how the war unfolded and how it ended, first for the French, and then for us twenty years later.

Johnson's original, instinctive analysis that it wasn't worth fighting for was dead right. However, more than anything in the world, Johnson wanted to be elected President in his own right. He was still in Kennedy's shadow. He felt beneath and intimidated by Kennedy's boys: McNamara and Bundy and the others. He feared most of all Kennedy's brother, Robert, whom he suspected, with good cause wanted to be President himself.

Unlike the four Presidents before him, Franklin or Harry or Dwight or John, Lyndon was not a warrior. He felt that lack acutely and the need to prove his manhood. He was under incredible pressure from the Joint Chiefs of Staff to flex America's military muscle, pressure from the presidential candidate trying to replace him, Barry Goldwater, who accused him of weakness toward the communists, pressure from the Catholic Church who wanted to keep those French-Indochina Catholics [xxx] they had created in that land of Buddhists. Most of all, he wanted to be elected in 1964 and reelected in 1968. He wasn't, in his words, "going to be the first American President to lose a war."

He should have listened to his instincts. He, of all people, should have known when he was being played. "Advisors advise but Presidents decide [my emphasis]." [xxiii] John Kennedy knew this. He had decided to reject the pro-military, anti-communist sentiment that had served him so poorly at the Bay of Pigs in 1961 and he probably saved the world from nuclear annihilation during the Cuban Missile crisis of 1962 by rejecting the military's recommendation to attack. He had already drafted the public position to scale back America's involvement in Vietnam before he was assassinated. At the end of 1963, just before President Kennedy was killed, there were 16,300 American military personnel in Vietnam, and he intended to reduce that number.

By the end of 1964, the US had 23,000 troops in Vietnam. President Johnson had won election against opposition from his left and his right and he had the Gulf of Tonkin Resolution in his pocket, empowering him to vastly increase the US troop commitment in Vietnam. By the end of 1965, Johnson had increased the troops to 184,000. By the time he left office, there were 536,000. At the peak of our troop deployment, in April 1969, President Nixon had increased the troop level to 543,000. When I got there in January 1970, the number had dropped back to 475,000. By the time I left in March of 1971, the number had dropped to less than 334,000. By the beginning of 1972, there were 156,000. By the end of 1972 it was 24,200 - about what it was when Johnson decided not to lose a war. At the end of 1973, the number was 50 and in April 1975 it was zero.

The net result was the same as if we had never picked the fight in the first place. Except for the fifty-eight thousand nine hundred and seventeen dead Americans, the quarter million wounded Americans, the 1.1 million enemy dead, the unknown number of dead and wounded civilians, the Americans missing in action to this day, and enough of our national treasure to build a highway to Mars.

The American troops did not fail in Vietnam. What they were asked to do was impossible and should never have been started. That they tried to do the impossible anyway is the height of loyalty and honor. That they were wasted is a national sin.

Endnotes

[i] The North Vietnamese Army (NVA) was the American name for our enemy from the north. The North Vietnamese called themselves the "People's Army of Vietnam (PAVN).

[ii] See "The Sons of Bardstown" by Jim Wilson, Crown Publishers, New York. Bardstown Kentucky was a small farming town in the bourbon belt that gained the horrible distinction of having the most Vietnam dead on a per capita basis in the country. "C" Battery was a Nation Guard unit in which all the men were from the same area, in and around the town of Bardstown, where everybody knew everybody else.

[iii] See "The Conflict that was a War", Chapter 11, pages 119-124 by Mark Tury, 1st Platoon, Charlie Company, 2/501st Infantry, 101st Airborne Division, who gives the grunts eye view of the June18th, 1969 attack on Tomahawk.

[iv] See The Sons of Bardstown, Chapter 3, "A Bad Hill".

[v] The M67 recoilless rifle M590 Antipersonnel Canister contains a payload of 2400, fin-stabilized, steel-wire darts.

[vi] More bombs were expended just on the Ho Chi Minh trail than all the bombs dropped in WWII.

[vii] From the French meaning "People from the mountains." These fierce fighters allied with the U.S. against the North Vietnamese.

[viii] See "Ripcord – Screaming Eagles Under Siege – Vietnam 1970" by Keith Nolan, Ballantine Books, 2003, and "Hell on a Hilltop" by General Benjamin Harrison, 2004. General Harrison returned to Vietnam in 2004 and met with the North Vietnamese General who commanded the forces who attacked Ripcord, giving him an unprece-

dented view of his former enemy's thinking and order of battle as well as access to the official PAVN archives in Hanoi. He was accompanied by my former Alpha Company Commander, Captain Fred Spaulding (now Lt. Col. Retired). Captain Spaulding is the purest warrior I have ever met. He was awarded the Distinguished Service Cross (the second highest Army medal that can be awarded) for his heroism during Operations Texas Star and especially the Siege of Ripcord when he commanded the air operations and particularly the successful rescue of the troops under fire there. He should have been awarded The Congressional Medal of Honor.

[ix] 101st Airborne Division Operational Report for period ending July 70, Page 1.

[x] Policy initiated by the Richard Nixon administration in January of 1969 to turn the war over to the Vietnamese so we could leave.

[xi] "In Retrospect", Robert McNamara, Vintage Books, 1996, page 84

[xii] "Blowing in the Wind", Song by Bob Dylan

[xiii] Hell on a Hilltop, page 41. This statistic of the 101st killing six or seven men for every ton of rice they stole from the villages is not American data but rather comes from the official North Vietnamese archives as detailed in General Harrison's book.

[xiv] They finally made us stop that after the Mai Lai Massacre became public in late 1969. It took another 6 months for the reality to sink in. After that, the SOP was to keep our distance from the boundaries of the villages themselves at night.

[xv] A soft headgear sometimes worn by the enemy. They also wore a pith helmet like the British wore in North Africa in WWII.

[xvi] "Hearts and Minds", a documentary film about the Vietnam War, directed by Peter Davis, 1974.

[xvii] See "Looking for a Hero – Joe Ronnie Hooper and the Vietnam War", Maslowski, University of Nebraska Press, 2004.

[xviii] Medal of Honor citation for HOOPER, JOE R. Rank and organization: Staff Sergeant, U.S. Army, Company D, 2d Battalion (Airborne), 501st Infantry, 101st Airborne Division. Place and date: Near Hue, Republic of Vietnam, 21 February 1968. Citation: For conspicuous gallantry and intrepidity in action at the risk of his life above and beyond the call of duty. Staff Sergeant (then Sgt.) Hooper, U.S. Army, distinguished himself while serving as squad leader with Company D. Company D was assaulting a heavily defended enemy position along a river bank when it encountered

a withering hail of fire from rockets, machineguns and automatic weapons. S/Sgt. Hooper rallied several men and stormed across the river, overrunning several bunkers on the opposite shore. Thus inspired, the rest of the company moved to the attack. With utter disregard for his own safety, he moved out under the intense fire again and pulled back the wounded, moving them to safety. During this act S/Sgt. Hooper was seriously wounded, but he refused medical aid and returned to his men. With the relentless enemy fire disrupting the attack, he single-handedly stormed 3 enemy bunkers, destroying them with hand grenade and rifle fire, and shot 2 enemy soldiers who had attacked and wounded the Chaplain. Leading his men forward in a sweep of the area, S/Sgt. Hooper destroyed 3 buildings housing enemy riflemen. At this point he was attacked by a North Vietnamese officer whom he fatally wounded with his bayonet. Finding his men under heavy fire from a house to the front, he proceeded alone to the building, killing its occupants with rifle fire and grenades. By now his initial body wound had been compounded by grenade fragments, yet despite the multiple wounds and loss of blood, he continued to lead his men against the intense enemy fire. As his squad reached the final line of enemy resistance, it received devastating fire from 4 bunkers in line on its left flank. S/Sgt. Hooper gathered several hand grenades and raced down a small trench which ran the length of the bunker line, tossing grenades into each bunker as he passed by, killing all but 2 of the occupants. With these positions destroyed, he concentrated on the last bunkers facing his men, destroying the first with an incendiary grenade and neutralizing 2 more by rifle fire. He then raced across an open field, still under enemy fire, to rescue a wounded man who was trapped in a trench. Upon reaching the man, he was faced by an armed enemy soldier whom he killed with a pistol. Moving his comrade to safety and returning to his men, he neutralized the final pocket of enemy resistance by fatally wounding 3 North Vietnamese officers with rifle fire. S/Sgt. Hooper then established a final line and reorganized his men, not accepting treatment until this was accomplished and not consenting to evacuation until the following morning. His supreme valor, inspiring leadership and heroic self-sacrifice were directly responsible for the company's success and provided a lasting example in personal courage for every man on the field. S/Sgt. Hooper's actions were in keeping with the highest traditions of the military service and reflect great credit upon himself and the U.S. Army.

[xix] "Looking for a Hero", Page 347

[xx] Telephone conversation between Lyndon Johnson and McGeorge Bundy, May 27th 1964, in Beschlos, Taking Charge, pp. 370-73. [From Lessons in Disaster, pp. 112-113]

[xxi] Peter MacDonald, "Giap: The Victor in Vietnam" (New York: W.W. Norton, 1993) p. 82. [From Lessons in Disaster, p. 50]

[xxii] "Lessons in Disaster, McGeorge Bundy and the Path to War in Vietnam", Gordon M. Goldstein, Time Books, 2008, Page 27.

ACKNOWLEDGEMENTS

My dear wife of 42 years, Laurie, line-edited every comma and misspelled word, and helped me clarify language for the non-military reader before I dared show any of this to an outsider.

I could not have written this book without the encouragement, support, and assistance of many friends, old and new. Rick Lehman and Bryon Runyon, my best friends from the Sanger High School Class of 1966, gave me the courage to go forward with a work I doubted, and gifted me with the first manuscript edits. I acknowledge with deep gratitude the inestimable help of Janice Stevens and the writers in her "Writing for Publication" class who listened to my drafts and gave me the feedback to make them better. My thanks also to my research assistant Lisa Farris who spent many hours chasing rabbits for me.

Most of all, I cannot thank enough my buddies from the 10st Airborne and especially the troopers of Alpha and Delta Companies who shared their experiences with me.

I also want to thank those troopers and others who generously shared their photographs with me including: Barney Barnes, Bill Beasley, Reagan Carosino*, Bob Cox, Bob Flannery, Roger Roy, Tim Rudd, Ed Schlappi, Frank Seeman, Gerald Seidl, Ray Sellers, Arvest Sparks, James Zuvar and others.

* (Reagan Carosino is the daughter of my friend Bryon Runyon. She visited Vietnam a few years ago to help orphans and gave me the picture of the cemetery below Tomahawk).

www.ingramcontent.com/pod-product-compliance
Lightning Source LLC
Chambersburg PA
CBHW021144080526
44588CB00008B/214